MY CHILDREN! MY AFRICA!
AND SELECTED
SHORTER PLAYS

ATHOL FUGARD

MY CHILDREN! MY AFRICA! AND SELECTED SHORTER PLAYS

Edited by Stephen Gray

 WITWATERSRAND UNIVERSITY PRESS

Witwatersrand University Press, PO Wits, Johannesburg 2050

First published 1990
Reprinted February 1991, May 1991

ISBN 1 86814 117 9

Set in 10pt Times by GraphicSet

Printed and bound by The Natal Witness Printing and Publishing Company (Pty) Ltd

"MY CHILDREN! MY AFRICA!"
Originally produced by The Market Theatre
in Johannesburg, June 1989

"THE DRUMMER"
Originally produced by
Actors Theatre of Louisville, Inc.

Contents

Introduction

This collection of plays by Athol Fugard has several obvious objectives.

At the Witwatersrand University Press it has been assembled and gone to print while his latest major theatrework has been enjoying its first run in the same city of Johannesburg. With Fugard's active encouragement, the script of *My Children! My Africa!* is now published in South Africa. As he has been quoted as saying by *Time* (on 10 July 1989), this one was "between me and my country". He has been true to his word and South Africa now has it first.

But the opportunity for Wits Press to bring out *My Children! My Africa!* coincided with another project: the completion of a long-overdue collection of Fugard plays that had not been in print, or at least were not easily accessible. There is no coincidence in the fact that most of the Fugard works that have 'disappeared' or become forgotten happen to be his short works. The commercial world of theatre and of script publication favours the longer and more readily consumable works; each provides an evening's entertainment and results in a marketable book.

The theory behind this volume of selected shorter plays was that throughout Fugard's career of the last three decades, he has as often as not found the unpopular short forms to be hospitable and amenable (no matter how 'non-commercial' they may be). One could even make a case for the shorter works being the very thought-tanks out of which the larger works have been developed and elaborated. After all, in the late 1950s, like so many of his contemporary English-language dramatists, Fugard began his first experiments in the one-act form. Since then he has persistently used related forms (like the film or TV play, the workshop experiment, and the improvised sketch). Such works may fit interstitially into the canon of larger works, but there are reasons why they should not be as ignored as they are. Firstly, the canon would not have the shape it has without them. Secondly, there can be no artistic grounds on which to uphold a belief that 'short' implies 'lesser'. On the contrary, Fugard seems naturally to be most at ease when working in compact, dense forms, and it is an orthodoxy of Fugard criticism that many of the works for which he is most renowned — like the collaborative *Sizwe Bansi is Dead* (1972) and *'Master Harold'... and the Boys* (1982) — are essentially expanded one-acters.

So the arrival of the script of that extremely large structure, *My Children! My Africa!* (but still... large enough for a fairly-priced single book?), signalled an ideal 'commercial' chance to bring the shorter selection into the durable and public format as well. Hence the strange shape of this collection.

The Occupation is a script for the camera. It was first published in the Cape Town journal, *Contrast*, as a substantial part of No. 8 of April 1964, and anthologised by Cosmo Pieterse in 1968 in his collection, *Ten One-act Plays*, in Heinemann Educational's African Writers Series. Fugard worked on *The Occupation* after *The Blood Knot* of 1961, while also writing *People are Living There* and *Hello and Goodbye*; in terms of environment and style of social realism, *The Occupation* could be said to share a common focus with these plays. It also deals with post-World War II poverty in South Africa in which marginalised whites gang up against dispossessed blacks, and uses all the claustrophobic menace of enclosed, dead-end living. Although written as a work for the camera, the abrasiveness of its content may have militated against a production for the cinema or television at the time. Fugard reworked similar material about a burglary in his successful feature film, *Marigolds in August*, some fifteen years later. With very little adaptation *The Occupation* could become a stage piece and, unlike many film scripts, it also reads fluently.

The second piece, *The Coat*, is devised for the stage — a bare stage — but under peculiar circumstances. Its subtitle, 'An Acting Exercise', needs the further qualification that it comes from the Serpent Players of New Brighton, the township in Port Elizabeth. This group of black performers, with whom Fugard worked intermittently as director during the second half of the 1960s, produced many performances of classic works, notably Sophocles' *Antigone* — which later became the play-within-the-play of *The Island* (1973) — and works by Machiavelli, Büchner, Beckett, Soyinka among others. Much of this period of Fugard's life, and of South African theatre in general, remains inadequately documented, particularly in regard to the extent to which such scripts became 'Africanised' to meet their environments of performance. But *The Coat* makes very clear the lines which this company pursued. It is derived from improvisation, and uses this as its main metaphor. It takes a story idea from Gogol's *The Overcoat*, using by-the-book Brechtian practice — subtitles, alienation and metacommentary included. But what *The Coat* also affected in the Serpent Players' repertoire was the use of locally relevant material. A political prisoner's mute token, related to all the dialectic of South African township being, is its central idea. *The Coat* sets a style of both social documentation and political provocation that matures in *Sizwe Bansi is Dead*, for example. The specifics of the script make its occasion self-explanatory. Although it was devised by Fugard and the performers to answer a theatrical need of a moment in Port Elizabeth in 1966 — and was first published in the Johannesburg review, *The Classic*, in 1977, to become one of the roots of black protest theatre at the time — as an experience in drama it reaches out far beyond those circumstances.

In 1968, in answer to a commission from the BBC, Fugard wrote the TV play, *Mille Miglia*, which at first sight is singularly uncharacteristic of his *oeuvre*, being one of the few works not set in his native South Africa. Yet the theme of *Mille Miglia* — endurance; trust between people in perilous circumstances; the push for survival and, in this case, winning; the obsessive care over details — be it on the part of a famous racing driver and his sidekick in a factual historical grand prix event or otherwise — smacks very much of Fugard's preoccupations of the time and subsequently. Its focus on a limited cast of characters under stress is typical. Produced in the same year, when TV techniques were not sufficiently developed for the camera to venture beyond interiors, it was also shot in colour, so that actual black-and-white footage of the original 1955 Mille Miglia race was excluded. This script ingeniously capitalised on the limitations of the technology

11

of the day. It has since been adapted, somewhat unsatisfactorily, for the stage as a two-hander (called *Drivers*), produced at the fringe Space Theatre in Cape Town in 1973. This script is a reading version of the original shooting script, transcribed with Fugard's own comments. It was first published in 1984 in an anthology called *Modern Stage Directions.*

Fugard's *Orestes*, first performed in Cape Town and Johannesburg in 1971, has long been one of his most controversial and even legendary works, chiefly for the odd reason that it was reputed to be — and some critics maintain still is — unscriptable. But if a script is no more than the blueprint from which a dramatic performance may be recreated, then we do have a full script of *Orestes* here. It was developed as the first project of a scratch 'Theatre Laboratory', with a modest state subsidy, by Fugard and a team of performers (including the actress 'Y' — Yvonne Bryceland) to experiment with the limits of theatre vocabulary. Although radical and drastic, its features include metatextuality (this time the *Oresteia*), non-verbal symbolism and violent explosion as central metaphor and as technique. *Orestes* is best experienced live or, failing that, on film. But Fugard has rendered it down into print, in the form of a letter to an absent friend. His source was all his original documentation as a scribe who filled multicoloured ledgers with copious charts and time scales. The *Orestes* experiment, through the use of Laing and Grotowski, blew open many of his 70s habits of using violent subtexts, classical underpinning and, above all, the most daring performer commitment, and led directly to the *Statements* group of plays that followed. This 'script', if it may now be accepted as such, first appeared in an anthology called *Theatre One: New South African Drama* in 1978 and then in *Theatre Quarterly*, London, in No. 32 of 1979, as its logical partner, the full-length *A Lesson from Aloes*, was opening in London and New York.

The next piece in this collection, *The Drummer*, is both the shortest of Fugard's works to date and one of his most life-asserting. Commissioned for the annual Festival of New American Plays of the Actors Theatre of Louisville, Kentucky, it was premièred in February 1980. Fugard's career truly moves in circuits within circuits, for in *The Drummer* we may see the characters of *The Occupation* revisited, but with a celebratory

12

sense of liberation which may indeed have much to do with his partial removal from South Africa to the United States. But the deftness, the intensely sharp theatrical-social moment, the succinct statement about art and its birth — all that remains. And now, two decades on, this has come to be called Fugardian. The script of *The Drummer* was first published in Russell Vandenbroucke's *Truths the Hand can Touch: The Theatre of Athol Fugard* in 1985.

By the time the reader comes to *My Children! My Africa!*, there is little to add. Echoes, cross-references, parallels with the other scripts here present abound. Just one example: the character Lavrenti (played by John Kani) said in *The Coat*, all those years back:

> We want to use the theatre... Some of us say to understand the world we live in but we also boast a few idealists who think that theatre might have something to do with changing it.

And now, as this volume emerges, those words of Kani resonate again in the latest script: so faithful to the stage in South Africa, so powerfully, undefeatably magnificent. .

Stephen Gray
February 1990

The Occupation

A Script for the Camera

Cast

BAREND
KOOSIE
SERGE
CAPPIE
— Four hoboes

First image: an old house. The camera is moving towards it along the weed-choked path of a neglected garden. Mood of dereliction and decay. The camera moves warily with shots from behind shrubbery and trees to suggest a stealthy approach.
Credits.
The camera reaches the house. A door with the doorknob missing, the paint cracked and peeling. A window either with shutters closed or boarded-up. The camera moves, as would a man, along a wall [shadows of men?] to another window, then another, then again a door... variations on the theme of an old house fallen into desuetude. Sound is natural — footsteps on gravel and cement, vague noises of attempts to prise open shutters, etc. In this opening scene and during the entry into the house the camera functions as a composite eye of the four men, showing us what they see. Our first sight of the men themselves will be, as indicated, in the lounge. Until that moment, all dialogue is off-screen.

KOOSIE'S VOICE: [*In the distance*] Ssst! Here. Captain! Over here!
    [*Shot changes abruptly to one of the windows which have already been passed. The shutters have been forced open. A dusty window pane, and through it a dim view of a small room.*]

SERGE'S VOICE: Go on!

KOOSIE'S VOICE: Captain?

CAPPIE'S VOICE: Okay.
    [*Camera focused on the window pane as it is smashed. Sound. As the glass breaks the shot again changes abruptly to:*
    Inside the room, which is seen from the position of the men who have just entered through the window. The camera is

17

stationary, but turning in a wide arc so that we see all of the room. Two doors. The room is bare. A few seconds of breathing silence at the start of this sequence, then, muffled by distance, a dove coos. This is also the cue for the following dialogue, which is heard while the camera turns slowly]:

KOOSIE'S VOICE: Captain...

CAPPIE'S VOICE: Sssh!

SERGE'S VOICE: There's no one. I tell you it's empty.

CAPPIE'S VOICE: Who's in charge here, Sergeant?

SERGE'S VOICE: Sorry, sir.

CAPPIE'S VOICE: [*Easier, a little louder*] Okay. It looks all right. You take that door, Sergeant. But watch out for booby-traps. Come on! [*Explosive, neurotic laughter from Sergeant*]

[*Camera moves forward to one of the two doors. During this move* SERGE'S *voice is heard from the other door.*]

SERGE'S VOICE: Must have been the kitchen. [*Pause*] No dice. Water's cut off.

[*On the last of* SERGE'S *words the shot changes to:*
The kitchen. Kitchen sink with taps; snarl of exposed wires where the stove stood against the wall; heap of rubbish — paper, dust, leaves — swept into one corner; on one wall a strip of wood with several nails for hanging up utensils. From one nail hangs an old piece of wire. While the camera is exploring the kitchen we hear the following dialogue from the other room]:

KOOSIE'S VOICE: It's tight, Captain. But it's not locked. I can see a big room.

CAPPIE'S VOICE: Mind. Barend!

BAREND'S VOICE: What? [*Sound of a violent blow*]

CAPPIE'S VOICE: That's it! [*A second and still more violent blow. On the sound of the second blow the camera cuts abruptly from the kitchen to the door which the camera approached earlier and which is now swinging open. The camera moves through into:*
A very large room, obviously the lounge in the days when the house was occupied. Again the wide swing of the camera, but this time travelling slowly to the centre of the room at the

same time. We see: A high, pressed-metal ceiling with two or three broken lengths of chain hanging where the light used to be; cobwebs in corners; somewhere on the floor the remains of a fire — ash and charred pieces of wood; dampstains on the walls with one or two places where the plaster has fallen away; a large marble-sided fireplace; windows and two glass-panelled double doors, all shuttered. Sunlight is streaming into the room through the latter. They face directly into the setting sun. This room is also bare, but in addition to the remains of the fire the floor is littered with other rubbish indicating occasional and vagrant occupants. There is a second doorway, but in this case the door itself is missing. As previously the following dialogue is heard while the camera establishes the room]:

KOOSIE'S VOICE: Hey!

CAPPIE'S VOICE: Easy does it, men! Easy does it!

SERGE'S VOICE: Booby-traps! [*Explosive laugh*]

CAPPIE'S VOICE: Sergeant!

SERGE'S VOICE: Sorry sir.

KOOSIE'S VOICE: Whose house is it, Captain?

SERGE'S VOICE: Who cares? It's empty.

KOOSIE'S VOICE: This was a big room, hey!

CAPPIE'S VOICE: The lounge. What's the bet? In the good old days.

SERGE'S VOICE: We're not the first.

CAPPIE'S VOICE: We won't be the last.

BAREND'S VOICE: So what we waiting for?

CAPPIE'S VOICE: Who's in command here, Private?

BAREND'S VOICE: Go to hell.

CAPPIE'S VOICE: Mark that man, Sergeant.

SERGE'S VOICE: Private Barend, sir.

CAPPIE'S VOICE: Mark him.

BAREND'S VOICE: [*Suddenly, shouting*] Hello! *Hello!* Anybody home?

[*On the second 'hello' an abrupt countershot showing the four men for the first time.*

They are hoboes: unshaven, unwashed, with down-at-heel shoes — one of them could have shoes but no socks — shapeless trousers and the same for whatever else they wear — sports coat, lumber jacket, or even just a pullover.

19

BAREND, *shouting, stand apart from the other three who are watching him. About thirty years old; a dark, brooding man, physically strong, even powerful. But as we see more of him, another impression will form — that of a strength that is inarticulate and lost. His broad shoulders should have been bent under the weight of hard work and those big hands — so empty! — shaping bricks into a wall, or digging. He is an Afrikaner and speaks English with difficulty.*

KOOSIE, *carrying a bundle, is the youngest. About twenty years old. He lives in a schizophrenic world, constantly straining to reconcile illusion and reality. A face, when not wide-eyed and eager, pinched into an anxious frown.*

SERGE *and* CAPPIE *are older men, approximately the same age — between forty-five and fifty.* SERGE *is holding the piece of wire last seen hanging in the kitchen. We have already heard him laugh. We will hear it again — a wild, mirthless sound thrown violently out of an open-mouthed face. More than anything else this expresses the man and his dominant mood: hypertension. He sweats a lot.*

CAPPIE *smiles slowly — expressive of his control over himself and the others, the situation. He is fascinated by the transience of all reality. I see him with greying hair and a moustache. He also has a tie — a small knot under a rumpled collar — and has a bottle of wine in each of his trouser pockets.*]

CAPPIE: Barend!

BAREND: [*Facing* CAPPIE] There's no one.

CAPPIE: That's mutiny, Private Barend. Men have been shot for less.

[SERGE *laughs*]

BAREND: Why don't you grow up?

CAPPIE: We're not finished. There's still the rest of the house.

SERGE: It is empty, Cap.

CAPPIE: They might have left something behind. Come on.
[*Fade to the hall which is beyond the second doorway. A staircase leads to the top floor. There are also a few doors leading off the hall to other rooms and the start of a passage.*]

KOOSIE: They must have been rich.

SERGE: Stinking rich if you ask me. Hey Cap?

CAPPIE: Wealth doesn't stink, Sergeant. It has a fine cultured aroma. Good cigars and scented bath-water.

[*As he starts to speak, and followed by* SERGE, CAPPIE *moves to the staircase.* KOOSIE *and* BAREND *stand motionless for a few seconds, listening and watching.*]

CAPPIE: [*Moving up the stairs*] Gracious living, my boys. That's what this was. Gracious living in the good old days. They had it good.

[KOOSIE *moves to one of the doors in the hallway.* BAREND *is alone for a few seconds.* KOOSIE *comes out.*]

KOOSIE: [*To* BAREND] Nothing.

[KOOSIE *goes into another room.* BAREND *now moves into the passage.*

Here follows a sequence alternating between CAPPIE *and* SERGE *upstairs,* KOOSIE *downstairs and* BAREND *in the passage. The latter image must be established strongly, both visually and aurally. There are broken windows along this passage and as a result leaves, now dry and rusty, cover the floor. These, and the pieces of glass breaking underfoot when he walks, will create a distinctive sound. But to start with, when* BAREND *moves into this passage we are given a stationary shot of its length. There is a door at the far end. No movement. Shot changes to:*

CAPPIE *and* SERGE *upstairs in an empty room.* CAPPIE *moves to a door in one of the walls, opens it and looks into another room.* SERGE *is drawing a heart with an arrow through it on a dusty window pane.*]

CAPPIE: Interleading door. Could have been the bedrooms. Yes. Mr and Mrs.

SERGE: Who?

CAPPIE: [*Smiles*] Yes.

SERGE: Mr and Mrs Who?

CAPPIE: That's it Serge, Mr and Mrs Who? Don't you get it?

SERGE: [*Blankly*] Mr and Mrs Who.

CAPPIE: Who were you? [*Walking away from the camera*] Who were you? Who Were You!

[*Followed by* SERGE, CAPPIE *moves deeper into the house. Shot changes to:*

21

Close-up, from inside a room, of KOOSIE *in the doorway. He is intent and watchful. Off-screen we hear the dry, feathered panic of beating wings.* KOOSIE *moves into the room, closing the door behind him. Takes a few steps into the room and then again stands still and watches. Shot changes to:*
CAPPIE *and* SERGE *in another room.*]

CAPPIE: And this? Let's see... yes. Yes.

SERGE: Well, come on.

CAPPIE: The nursery.

SERGE: How do you know?

CAPPIE: The walls... that wallpaper. And it gets the afternoon sun. Just the place for the little mites.

SERGE: Know your way around, hey Cap!

CAPPIE: I'm in tune with the past, Sergeant.

KOOSIE'S VOICE: [*Muffled*] Captain! Captain!

CAPPIE: They're most probably still alive.

SERGE: The kids.

CAPPIE: This, Serge, is another man's memory, and what's the bet he hates it.

KOOSIE'S VOICE: [*Louder*] Captain!

[CAPPIE *and* SERGE *turn and leave in response to* KOOSIE'S *calling. Shot changes to:*
Hallway. Camera at top of stairs, focused on KOOSIE *at the bottom.*]

CAPPIE: [*Off-screen*] Find anything?

KOOSIE: In there, Captain.

[*Shot changes to:*
The passage. BAREND *has reached the door. It opens, but just before we can see what is beyond it there is a change to a countershot of* BAREND'S *face, in close-up. This is held for a few seconds. He is staring at something. Off-screen we hear muffled, indistinct dialogue between* KOOSIE, SERGE *and* CAPPIE. *Without either* BAREND *or the camera moving, this shot changes to:*
KOOSIE'S *room. He,* CAPPIE *and* SERGE *are all looking up at something. The sound of beating wings. Eyes and heads move.*]

KOOSIE: It's wild. It's trying to get out.

SERGE: Cappie! Pigeon pie! [*Laughs*]

KOOSIE: It's not a pigeon, it's a dove.

SERGE: Just a joke.

KOOSIE: Must I catch it, Captain?

CAPPIE: Yes. Yes, catch it.

[KOOSIE *moves forward into the camera. Shot changes to: The passage. The camera is positioned outside the door which is now wide open. Through the door, inside a small room, we see* BAREND, *his back to the camera, moving towards an old iron bed with a piece of mattress on its sagging springs. When he reaches the bed he moves to the head and looks down at it so that we see him in profile. He holds this position for a few seconds until a mumble of dialogue from the other three makes him look sharply at the door — that is, straight into the camera. The off-screen murmur continues.* BAREND *moves suddenly, straight to the camera which in turn starts backing down the passage.* BAREND *closes the door and hurries furtively down the passage. The camera is backing all the time, but slower so that he eventually moves into it when the shot changes to:* KOOSIE *holding the dove.*]

SERGE: Just an old dove.

KOOSIE: What must I do with it, Captain?

SERGE: Why? It's harmless. Eats flies.

KOOSIE: Maybe it carries messages for them.

SERGE: Who?

KOOSIE: The enemy.

[CAPPIE *and* SERGE *in close-up while* KOOSIE *talks. They watch him with vacant fascination.*]

KOOSIE: [*Off-screen*] Reinforcements. They need reinforcements. Isn't that so, Captain? And the doves carries the message.

SERGE: [*Winking*] Better take it prisoner then. Hey, Cap?

KOOSIE: And then?

CAPPIE: We'll decide later. Leave it here.

[KOOSIE *releases the dove. They back out of the room;* KOOSIE *closes the door on the camera. Slow fade on the closed door as seen from inside the room. Sound of the bird's wings.*

In the lounge. Shot of the second doorway as SERGE, CAPPIE *and* KOOSIE *enter. They stop and stare. Counter-shot of the room showing* BAREND *sitting on the floor at the far end, his back to the wall, playing with the piece of wire* SERGE *found in the kitchen.*]

CAPPIE: [*Off-screen*] Find anything?

BAREND: [*Without looking up*] Nothing.

[KOOSIE *moves into the frame and sits beside* BAREND.]

KOOSIE: [*To* BAREND] I found a dove in the other room. It's alive. We've taken it prisoner. We decide its fate later.

CAPPIE: [*Off-screen*] Nothing?

BAREND: [*Still not looking up*] Nothing.

[*Shot changes to* CAPPIE *alone at the door.* SERGE *has also moved into the room.*]

CAPPIE: Nothing. [*Slow smile*] How do you like that! Nothing. [*Moving forward, looking around the room*] Nothing! Not a fuck.

[*Shot changes to* SERGE *sitting on the floor, watching* CAPPIE. CAPPIE *will not be seen again until the speech starting "It was real".*]

SERGE: Remember that one in Italy? Near Monte Cassino? [*Speaking across the room to* BAREND] Cappie says it was a palace. Paintings on the ceiling. Life size.

CAPPIE: [*Off-screen*]... Last year's leaves and other men's rubbish...

SERGE: [*Still to* BAREND] Did it on his back. Lying down. One of those Italian names. Cappie knows all about it. [*Sudden vacancy; to himself*] Monte Cassino! Jesus.

[*Shot changes to* BAREND, *still playing with the wire.*]

CAPPIE: [*Off-screen*] Look at it! In rooms like this men... men dream! You dream! The generations to come... in the lovely old house that Jack built.

BAREND: I'm hungry...

CAPPIE: [*Off-screen*] Or the future. That's their word. The future! They sat...

BAREND: Let's eat.

KOOSIE: [*Busy with his bundle*] Fish and chips. There was also enough for cream cakes again. But they got squashed.

BAREND: [*Betraying a nervousness*] Okay, so let's eat.

KOOSIE: I still got to get water.

CAPPIE: [*Off-screen*]... fat backsides and talked and dreamt...

24

[*Shot changes back to* SERGE.]

SERGE: [*Still in the vacancy of his previous line*] Once is enough. [*Breaking mood*] Hey Barend! Heard this one? "The cradle of ancient civilisation." [*Laughs*] Cappie said it.

CAPPIE: [*Off-screen*] Sergeant! Where's your respect for the dead?

SERGE: Sorry sir.

[*Shot changes to* KOOSIE, *looking up from his bundle at* CAPPIE.]

CAPPIE: [*Off-screen*] Because they're dead. It's finished. Nothing's left. This was the future.

[*Shot changes to* BAREND, *who for the first time in this sequence also looks at* CAPPIE.]

CAPPIE: [*Off-screen*] The four of us. In here. Now! Do you get it? Use your imagination, you nits!

[*Shot changes to a long shot of the room, taking in all four men — the three sitting on the floor and* CAPPIE *standing. A camera angle that will suggest space and emptiness.*]

CAPPIE: It was real! Solid! They could touch it. Smell it. See it. Look! Tables and chairs... armchairs; pictures on the walls; carpets on the floor! And the noise! The laughing and crying, the whispers wrapped up in these walls! Are you deaf? The air in here was so thick with living it choked them! [*Pause*] But the clocks were ticking. They were warned. Waking at night, in the neither today, nor yesterday, nor yet tomorrow. A moment in a sleeping house... except... what is that? You listen hard. Yes. The old clock ticking away on the landing. Ticking. That's all. Ticking away. They never sound quite the same in the light. And then, just for a moment, one seasick little moment, it seems that everything is floating. You, your bed, the walls, the house itself... all gently drifting together... for the moment. Because there are no anchors. Nothing is heavier than time, my boys. Everything floats, and one day, maybe just as gently, you and your bed, and the walls...

[*Cut abruptly to* BAREND. *He throws away the wire — a strong deliberate gesture to break the mood. His next line cuts* CAPPIE'S *speech.*]

BAREND: I said I'm hungry.

SERGE: [*Off-screen*] Captain, there's a man here reports he's hungry.

[*Shot changes to* KOOSIE, *anxious-faced as he follows the next few lines of dialogue, all of which is off-screen.*]

CAPPIE: Mark him.

SERGE: Private Barend, sir.

CAPPIE: Mark him.

SERGE: Private Barend, step forward!

BAREND: For Christ's sake, grow up.

[*Shot changes to* BAREND, *with* CAPPIE *squatting on his haunches in front of him.*]

CAPPIE: What's the matter, Barend? You look worried.

BAREND: Since when?

CAPPIE: Never been in a house like this before? You weren't listening to me. Nobody's left to see your table manners. [SERGE *laughs.*]

BAREND: Why don't you drop dead for a change?

CAPPIE: You don't like me. Why, Barend! I try my best. Aren't you happy with us? You can always go.

BAREND: You finished?

CAPPIE: Yes. [*Pause*] You finished too? [SERGE *laughs*] All right chaps. Let's count the kitty.

[*The four men squat down.* KOOSIE *has a cigar box.*]

KOOSIE: I think it was a good day.

SERGE: [*Taking money out of his pocket*] Not so bad.

CAPPIE: Was it a good day, Barend?

BAREND: It was okay.

CAPPIE: Okay? [*Holding a handful of coins under Barend's nose.*] Don't you call that a good day?

SERGE: How do you do it, Cap? Rob them?

CAPPIE: I appeal to their better natures. [*To* BAREND] How did you make out?

BAREND: I did okay. [*Now also has his money out, but he keeps his hand closed*]

[*There is a tension between* BAREND *and* CAPPIE, *watching each other like players in a poker game.* CAPPIE *is confident;* BAREND *hides fear behind a mask of stubborn indifference.*]

CAPPIE: I hope so, because I think it's time we paid dues again. Isn't that so, quartermaster?

KOOSIE: Yes, Captain.

CAPPIE: [*Placing two half-crowns on the floor in front of* KOOSIE] Come on. Five bob all round. We don't want any bums in this group — do we, Barend?
[SERGE *puts down his five shillings, made up of two florins and a shilling.* KOOSIE *puts down a florin, two shillings and two sixpences.* BAREND *counts the money in his hand, holding it so that the others can't see.* CAPPIE *watches him intently. Eventually* BAREND *puts down a collection of coins — a shilling piece, sixpences, tickeys and pennies.*]

CAPPIE: Pennies! [*To* KOOSIE, *indicating Barend's contribution*] Count it, quartermaster. [*To* BAREND] Looks like you just made it.

BAREND: I did okay.

SERGE: But you frighten them. He frightens them, Cappie.

CAPPIE: You must smile, Barend. Learn to say 'please'.

BAREND: I did okay.

KOOSIE: [*Indicating Barend's money*] Five bob, sir.

BAREND: [*Trying to get away*] Let's eat.

CAPPIE: [*Enjoying himself*] We're not finished. How we off for stores, quartermaster?

KOOSIE: [*Putting the money away in a cloth tobacco bag*] I think we need more shoelaces, Captain. [*Opens the cigar box to reveal a few pairs of shoelaces*] Yes, sir. There's only four left.

CAPPIE: [*Places two shilling piece on the floor*] You know the rules. Come. [*Watches* BAREND *intently.* SERGE *and* KOOSIE *make their contribution*] We're waiting, Barend. [BAREND *counts the money in his hand*] What's wrong? [BAREND *opens his hand*] Five pence!

BAREND: I'll give you my share tomorrow...

CAPPIE: No, you won't! Nobody stays in the group on credit. We agreed.

SERGE: You frighten them. That's your trouble.

CAPPIE: [*To* BAREND] So?

BAREND: I don't know.

CAPPIE: The rules are that when a man can't make an equal contribution to stores or pay his dues, then he must leave the group.

BAREND: I don't care.

27

SERGE: Hell, Cappie!

CAPPIE: [*Sudden flash of anger*] What do you mean... 'Hell, Cappie!'

SERGE: Just... you know... hell, man...

CAPPIE: If you've got something to say, say it.

SERGE: I'll lend him two bob.

CAPPIE: The rules forbid credit within the group! I didn't make them. You wanted them. You made them.

SERGE: I'll give him two bob. A present.

CAPPIE: Give!... A present! What the hell do you think you are?

KOOSIE: [*Consulting a piece of paper*] Captain... the shoelaces left is still all Barend's share. He didn't give any away since the last lot.

CAPPIE: [*Looking at* BAREND] He didn't give any away?

KOOSIE: No, sir.

CAPPIE: [*To* BAREND] Then you're a bum.

BAREND: They don't want to take them.

CAPPIE: You're a bum.

SERGE: Don't frighten them, Barend. Watch Cappie next time. Smile at them.

CAPPIE: One of these days, Barend...

BAREND: So? You think I care?

CAPPIE: Yes! I don't know why. But you care!

[*The sun is beginning to set outside — a strong dazzle of light through the shutters of the double doors reflecting a pattern of shadows on the walls and ceiling.*]

KOOSIE: Be dark just now. Must I get things ready, Captain?

CAPPIE: Yes. [*His moment with* BAREND *is past.* CAPPIE *sits back against the wall next to* SERGE.]

SERGE: This could be cosy, you know, Cap.

KOOSIE: I still got to get water.

SERGE: Remember that tank in the yard? And some wood for a fire! Hey, Cap? On the double, Private Koosie.

[KOOSIE *leaves the room. During the sequence that now follows* BAREND *will be in focus almost all the time... showing increasing restlessness and tension. The effect of the setting sun — light through the shutters and reflections on the wall — will rise to a climax and then fade.*

To start with, while SERGE *is talking (the speech which*

28

follows), BAREND *lights a cigarette and smokes it for a few seconds. Then he stands up and moves halfway across the room to the doorway to the hall, stops, changes direction and goes instead to one of the double doors. He looks out through the shutters at the setting sun. All the time* SERGE'S *voice rambles on off-screen.*]

SERGE: [*Off-screen*] Easily make this cosy, Cap. Set ourselves up for a few days. Remember that place in Doornfontein? Two weeks, Barend. Two whole bloody weeks. The water turned on and one room had a light. Lavatory, the lot. Old Whitey was still with us. What about it, Cap? Nobody saw us. They wouldn't mind if we kept it clean. H.Q. for future operations.[*He laughs*] Old geezer this morning. Did I tell you? Offered me a job. "No charity my good man, but if you are prepared to do a day's honest work..." *"Go and drop dead!"* Should have seen his face! *"Stuff your job where the monkey stuffs his nuts!"*
[*At this point* BAREND *sits down on the floor. Change to a counter-shot of* CAPPIE *and* SERGE *sitting against the opposite wall.* SERGE *is talking to* CAPPIE. CAPPIE *is watching* BAREND.]

SERGE: [*Mimicking an old man's voice*] "Tramp... a... a vulgar hobo... I .. I'll call the police!" "You know what you and the police can do," I said. You listening, Cap?

CAPPIE: I'm listening.

SERGE: I told him begging comes from the Bible. Any case, with the shoelaces it's not begging, hey Cap? The police can't arrest us. We give something in return.

CAPPIE: That's the whole point.

SERGE: Exactly. That's the whole point. And what about what they owe us? Hey, Barend! Heard this one. "Society's debt to the gallant boys with the orange flash." [*Violent laugh*] Smuts. Didn't he say that, Cappie?

CAPPIE: I was there.

SERGE: What did I tell you? Should have joined up, Barend. It helps sometimes. Especially old ladies. They remember.

CAPPIE: He says he was too young.
[CAPPIE *and* SERGE *stare silently at* BAREND *for a few seconds. Camera returns to* BAREND. *In this silence he*

29

stands up and moves to the other double-door where he again
stares out at the sunset. We begin to feel it desolates him.
The following dialogue is again off-screen.]

SERGE: You know something, Cap?

CAPPIE: What?

SERGE: I'm glad we didn't go on the road this winter. And you?
Durban's fine, but the road gets me down, man. I never
liked it, you know. Even Durban's bad enough, but Cape
Town! Shit-a-brick! Now, let's see... one... two... three,
with old Hoppy... four... five. Five times. It's hell this
time of the year. Those thunderstorms in the Karoo...
[*During this speech another sound is heard — very faint at*
first, but growing steadily stronger. It is soon identified as
the sound of BAREND *walking down the passage — the dry*
leaves and broken glass underfoot. As it grows louder,
SERGE'S *voice gets softer until his line "Thunderstorms in the*
Karoo..." is just audible. For a few seconds after this
SERGE *mumbles on indistinctly while the sound of* BAREND'S
footsteps is heard loud and clear. The camera remains on
BAREND *all the time. The idea, of course, is that* BAREND *is*
hearing those footsteps, that he is re-experiencing his finding
of the bed.
In other words something intensely personal is happening to
him. We sense the contours of a blind and desperate hope.
The function of the camera is to find this and relate it to the
physical reality of the man — the old shoes; the coarse,
calloused, empty hands; the unlovable face.
The sound-illusion and mood are broken by SERGE'S
characteristic laugh, following which his voice is heard again
at normal strength.]

SERGE: [*Off-screen*] But it's fact! It could drive a man mad. Rain
on a corrugated iron roof. The Russians use it. Put a
bucket on your head and hit it with broomsticks. Five
minutes and you're loco. The noise does it. Hoppy read an
article. Anyway, I just stood there on the road and got
wet. Jesus, it came down! Hailstones, the lot. Hoppy says
I was crying, but I couldn't tell with the rain running
down my face. When it stopped we went back inside. It
was a squeeze. They're only small you know. Spent the

night there...

[About halfway through the above speech the sound illusion — the footsteps — starts again. But this time there is also a visual illusion. As they grow in volume and SERGE'S *voice gets softer, the shot of* BAREND *dissolves slowly into a shot of the bed which he found in the little room at the end of the passage. The bed is seen as* BAREND *must have seen it: first from the door, the camera then travelling up to it and finally moving around to the head.* BAREND *is not seen. Just the bed. There is also no sound — the footsteps fade out with the dissolve.*

This image is going to be shattered by CAPPIE'S *voice. But instead of a simple dissolve or cut back to the reality of* BAREND *at the double-door, the image — the bed — should break up as if it were being seen through a pane of glass which is broken at the appropriate moment, as happened with the window pane at the start of the play. The two moments are parallel in meaning. The change comes on* CAPPIE'S *second "Barend!"]*

CAPPIE: *[Off-screen]* Barend! Barend!

[Shot of BAREND *— a moment of confusion.]*

CAPPIE: *[Off-screen, this time softly; sweetly]* Barend!

[As BAREND *turns his head the shot changes to:* CAPPIE *and* SERGE. SERGE *is still sitting against the wall, watching* BAREND *and laughing. But* CAPPIE *is now standing a few steps in front of* SERGE.]*

CAPPIE: Starting up again, is it?

BAREND: What?

CAPPIE: That's what I'd like to know. *[Moving to* BAREND]* What is it Barend? What happens?

SERGE: Confide in your commanding officer.

BAREND: I don't know what you are talking about.

CAPPIE: Don't you.

BAREND: I... I was thinking.

CAPPIE: Thinking. I see. Well, I'm talking about the sunset...and you. Always at sunset. I've noticed. You watch it.

BAREND: Why can't I watch it?

CAPPIE: I'm not saying you can't watch it.

BAREND: So what you trying to prove?

31

CAPPIE: I'm not trying to prove anything.

BAREND: Because if you think I'm scared or something...

CAPPIE: Who said anything about being scared? Take Serge now — he's scared. Of the dark. I think he believes in ghosts.

SERGE: Bulldust.

CAPPIE: With you it's... it's... you know the feeling I get sometimes watching you, Barend? I get the feeling you're lonely.

BAREND: Look, there's nothing. Nothing happens. You're talking a lot of rubbish.

CAPPIE: [*Quietly*] You know that's a lie. [*To the shutters. He looks out*] The sun sets. It gets colder... darker... and shadows. They're different, aren't they Barend? Grey. Old. It's an old world. They come at us like scavengers. [*Changing mood, cheerfully*] You know where you'd be happy, Barend? The land of the midnight sun.

SERGE: [*Laughing*] You're a bullduster, Cap. Mid... night... sun!

CAPPIE: Think of it, man. It doesn't set. Twenty-four hours of sunshine.

SERGE: That a fact, Cappie?

CAPPIE: But there's a catch. Six months later the old bastard doesn't come up at all! That would do it, hey! A whole day of night!

KOOSIE: [*Off-screen and in the distance, but getting louder*] Captain. Captain. Captain!

CAPPIE: That would put the fat in the fire!

[*Enter* KOOSIE *out of breath. At first* CAPPIE *ignores him.*]

CAPPIE: [*To* BAREND] Got your candle? Use it tonight. Wind doesn't blow in here.

KOOSIE: [*Agitated*] Captain. Please, sir!

SERGE: O.C.'s busy, Private. What do you want? And stand to attention!

KOOSIE: The enemy, Serge. Coming to the house.

SERGE: [*Urgently*] Cappie!

CAPPIE: What?

KOOSIE: The enemy, please sir, Captain. He's coming to the house.

CAPPIE: Who?

KOOSIE: A native. He's carrying a knobkerrie.

CAPPIE: [*Moving*] At the back?

KOOSIE: No Captain. There. The front. Where's our guns, Sergeant?

[*All four to the shutters. They look out. When they speak again it is in whispers.*]

CAPPIE: Watchman.

KOOSIE: What must we do, Captain? Where's our guns?

SERGE: [*Note of panic*] Will you shut up about guns? We haven't got ...

CAPPIE: Easy, easy, easy, Serge!

SERGE: I hate this.

BAREND: Maybe he won't come in. [*Pause*]

SERGE: [*Rising note of panic; backing away from the double-door*] No. No!! No! He's coming!!

[*The others also back away, then turn and move.*

Now follows a sequence showing their silent, tiptoed panic and flight through the house. To begin with, the lounge; KOOSIE *moves to his bundle and hurriedly collects everything together;* BAREND *makes for the doorway leading to the hall;* SERGE *has backed into a wall and stands rigid.*]

CAPPIE: [*As* KOOSIE *also moves to the hall*] Not that way! Come back. [*To* SERGE, *whom he gives a violent shove*] Snap out of it! Move. The back window.

[SERGE *rushes off through the first door.* CAPPIE, *also at the door, turns around.*]

CAPPIE: Koosie! Barend! The back window!

[*Counter-shot of the empty lounge. A sudden high-pitched scream tears the heavy silence. It is* SERGE'S *voice imitating a falling bomb. Starts on a high note and then slides down the scale, followed by an imitation of the explosion. Again and again.*]

CAPPIE: Shit! [*He turns sharply and appears through the door*]

[*Series of shots showing the four men in different parts of the house — each shot lasting only a few seconds.* KOOSIE *is scampering up the stairs;* BAREND, *in the passage, armed with a heavy stick, turns to face the camera in a defensive attitude;* CAPPIE, *moving through the house looking for* SERGE; *and* SERGE, *in close-up, crouched somewhere, his face twisted, hands protecting his head, screaming. This*

33

scream is the only sound; muffled and remote in the shot of
KOOSIE *and* BAREND, *louder with* CAPPIE, *and immediate
and real during the shots of* SERGE.
Then, during a shot of KOOSIE, *hiding at the top of the
stairs, a silence as sudden as was the start of the screaming.
Quick cut to a shot of* BAREND, *stick in his hand, waiting.
Then a shot of* CAPPIE *and* SERGE, *now together.* CAPPIE *has
his hand over* SERGE'S *mouth.*
Silence. The dove coos.
KOOSIE *and* BAREND *are seen again — so motionless the
frames could be stills. Camera returns to* CAPPIE *and* SERGE.
*Off-screen a furtive sound (footsteps?). Counter-shot of the
door as it opens.* KOOSIE *appears. Camera stays on* KOOSIE
until he leaves.]

KOOSIE: He's gone.
CAPPIE: [*Off-screen*] What are you staring at?
KOOSIE: Sergeant...
CAPPIE: [*Off-screen*] Find Barend.
KOOSIE: Is Sergeant...?
CAPPIE: I said find Barend!
KOOSIE: Yes, sir.

> [KOOSIE *turns and leaves: Shot changes to:*
> CAPPIE *and* SERGE. CAPPIE *still has his hand over* SERGE'S
> *mouth.*]

CAPPIE: Let go. [SERGE *relaxes.* CAPPIE *takes his hand away.*]
SERGE: They never give you a chance, hey!
CAPPIE: Never.
SERGE: Sudden. Like bombs.
CAPPIE: It's always sudden.
SERGE: Cap, I... [*He stops*] Don't laugh.
CAPPIE: I won't.

> [SERGE *is limp, damp with sweat, almost on the verge of
> tears.* CAPPIE *plays out this moment with a front of non-
> committal indifference but behind it we feel...*]

SERGE: I just wanted to be happy. Truly. All my life... that's all
I wanted. [*Pause*] Do you know what I mean, Cap?
[*Pause*] Is that too much?
CAPPIE: No. [*Examines one of his fingers*]
SERGE: What's that?

34

CAPPIE: You were biting me.

SERGE: Monte Cassino.

CAPPIE: I know.

SERGE: Anyway, he's gone. [*Starting to laugh*] He's gone, Cap!

CAPPIE: [*Smiling*] And we're still alive.

[*Shot changes to: The passage.* KOOSIE *at one end, the camera on* BAREND *at the other.*]

KOOSIE: It's okay now. He's gone. [*Pause*] Come. [*Pause*] Did you you hear Serge? He ... [*Stops*] That funny noise. It was him. In the kitchen. He ... he ... [*Pause*] Come. Captain said you must come.

[*The camera starts to move to* KOOSIE. *Fade.*
The lounge. SERGE *is sitting on the floor, whistling and playing with the piece of wire he found in the kitchen.*
CAPPIE *has taken out one of his bottles of wine and is drinking. There is a subtle change — the excitement has sharpened him, given a keen edge to his eyes and smile. This will be heightened by the wine.* KOOSIE *comes in from the hall.*]

CAPPIE: Where's Barend?

KOOSIE: Coming, Captain.

CAPPIE: What was he doing?

KOOSIE: Waiting.

CAPPIE: Was he frightened?

KOOSIE: He had a stick. If I had a gun, Captain, I could have killed that kaffir. He didn't see me.

[BAREND *comes into the lounge. He still has his stick — it comes from a fire which other vagrants had made in the house. One end is charred.*]

SERGE: Sa-loo ... oot Arms! All present and accounted for, sir. No casualties.

KOOSIE: [*Joining* SERGE] I was up top there by the stairs. I could have taken a pot shot at him. Sitting duck.

SERGE: Get the grub. Battle makes a man hungry.

KOOSIE: Must we still bivouac here, Captain?

SERGE: Why not? He didn't see us.

KOOSIE: Maybe he heard us. You were making that noise.

SERGE: [*Defensive ignorance*] What noise?

KOOSIE: That funny noise.

SERGE: Bulldust.

KOOSIE: And he's gone to call the police! Remember that other place.

SERGE: What do you think, Cappie?

[*Shot of* CAPPIE *with his bottle.*]

CAPPIE: He might have heard you.

BAREND: [*Off-screen*] I'm staying.

[*Cut to shot of* BAREND.]

KOOSIE: Captain gives the orders.

BAREND: Nobody gives me orders!

KOOSIE: Mustn't fight with me, we're in the same outfit.

BAREND: You can do what you like. I'm staying.

[*Shot changes to* CAPPIE *watching* BAREND.]

CAPPIE: Who's that brave man, Sergeant?

SERGE: Private Barend, sir. A credit to the regiment. [*Laugh*]

KOOSIE: Captain?

CAPPIE: We'll stay.

KOOSIE: I'll get water.

CAPPIE: [*Moving to* BAREND] Taken a shine to this spot. Feeling at home now.

BAREND: Ek is nie bang vir 'n—

CAPPIE: Speak English!

BAREND: I don't run from a kaffir.

CAPPIE: But you did, Barend! We were running. All of us. Serge had a dose of the jitters. Me too. Koosie. And you. Yes! You got out of here like all hell was behind you. We were scared. Fear, Barend, fear! And then hate. Them. Theirs. They hate us. Even dead they hate us. It wasn't that nigger. It's not his house. It's them . . . witmense like us.

[SERGE *is laughing,* CAPPIE, *smiling, takes a drink from his bottle.* BAREND *is rigid with suppressed emotion. Then he moves abruptly, crossing the room to the wall with the door through which they first entered the lounge. With the charred piece of firewood he starts to scrawl an obscenity on the wall. Enormous letters.* KOOSIE *appears in the doorway with a bottle of water.* BAREND *gets as far as FUC when the shot changes to* CAPPIE *and* SERGE, *watching him.* CAPPIE *has a detached, ironic smile.* SERGE *is concentrating, spelling out the letters under his breath. When he gets the message he starts to laugh, violently.* KOOSIE *moves into his frame.*]

KOOSIE: [*To* SERGE] What's he doing?

SERGE: Look!

[*Shot of* BAREND *scrawling another obscenity. Shot changes back to* SERGE *and* KOOSIE.]

KOOSIE: What is it?

SERGE: Can't you read?

[*Cut back to* BAREND. *He has finished and throws away the piece of wood, then looks defiantly at* CAPPIE.]

CAPPIE: [*Moving up to* BAREND] You also write on lavatory walls, don't you? Yes. I know your sort. [*Examines the writing on the wall*] You've just insulted the dead. Why? Because they're helpless.

[*Cut to* KOOSIE *and* SERGE.]

KOOSIE: [*To* SERGE] Who? [SERGE *starts whistling vigorously*]

[*Cut back to* CAPPIE *and* BAREND.]

CAPPIE: Answer me, damn you! Why did you do that?

BAREND: Because I don't care about them or their house. They're dead. It's empty. Tonight I'm . . .

CAPPIE: No Barend! No! You care! [*The writing on the wall*] That proves it. I thought it was empty but you . . . you feel something in here, don't you?

[*Shot of* KOOSIE *and* SERGE. KOOSIE *is listening seriously to the dialogue between* CAPPIE *and* BAREND. SERGE *is trying not to hear it.*]

SERGE: Where's the food?

KOOSIE: Is there ghosts here, Serge?

SERGE: Dry up, won't you! Get the grub.

KOOSIE: Captain hasn't said anything . . .

SERGE: Well, I'm second in command and I'm telling you to get the grub. For Christ's sake!

[*Shot changes to* CAPPIE *and* BAREND.]

CAPPIE: A home? Is that it? Can you still smell a home in here, Barend? You're keen, man. I missed it. Yes, we're pissing all over the memory of a happy home. We're not even trespassers. We're defilers. And you're jealous. That's what that means [*The obscenity*]. This is theirs and you're jealous. Are you that broke? If we kicked you out,

37

wouldn't you have anywhere to go?

BAREND: You think I'm hard up for you?

CAPPIE: I hope not. Be hell for you if you were.

BAREND: I'll go my own way any time. The lot of you can get...

CAPPIE: Yes, yes. You've got it on the wall. We've all
read it. And remember, so have they.

KOOSIE: Is there ghosts here, Captain?

CAPPIE: Do you hear that, Barend? Tell him. I feel
them now.

BAREND: You're talking rubbish. [*Moves away*]

SERGE: Yes, knock it off, Cap.

CAPPIE: Do you also feel them, Serge? It's worse
when they're dead, isn't it? Barend sees them.

SERGE: For the last time, is that food ready, Koosie?

KOOSIE: [*Correcting him*] Private Koosie.

SERGE: Private be damned!

KOOSIE: Hey!

SERGE: Yes, Private be damned! Wake up for Christ's sake.

CAPPIE: Serge is frightened of ghosts.

SERGE: For crying out aloud...!

CAPPIE: Watch it, Serge. Watch it. [*To* BAREND] See what
you've done? How many of them, Barend? One? Two?
Three? Where?... There! Yes? Help me, Barend. A man or
a woman? No! It's a little girl. A pretty little girl... with
her dolly. Don't be frightened girlie. Come to the nice old
man. [SERGE *laughs violently.* CAPPIE *pretends suddenly to
see someone else*] Madam! Our humble apologies. Didn't
know... you'd be home. Ex-servicemen, Lady.
Honourable discharge. Down on our luck. Could I interest
you in a pair of shoelaces... black shoelaces. You see,
Lady, we're not beggars. Small matter of shelter though.
We'll doss on the floor and piss in the garden. Promise!
But you see, Madam, we've forgotten what beds are like,
but we do remember roofs. God bless you, Lady. And
your little girl... God bless you both! [*Turning to the
others*] Boys, the lady says we can sleep on the floor.
[*Three quick close-ups of* BAREND, *who says nothing, then*
SERGE *and* KOOSIE.]

SERGE: [*Blankly*] Thank you, Ma'am. [*Then a laugh*]

KOOSIE: [*Uncertain*] Who... who...? Thank you, lady.
  [*Camera back to* CAPPIE.]
CAPPIE: Barend! Where's your respect! These people were
  your betters. They've given you shelter for the night.
  [*Turning to the imaginary presence*] Watch him, lady. A
  bad eff. Keep your little girl away from him and lock the
  door tonight.
BAREND: I wasn't born yesterday you know. There's
  nothing. This is just an empty house... and I'm going to
  stay here because I want to... and no kaffir chases me
  away. So, julle kan gaan bars!
CAPPIE: [*Drinking*] Something's worrying you.
  [*We now see* KOOSIE *preparing their supper on a sheet of
  newspaper. There is a bottle of water, the fish and chips and
  four cream cakes. The following dialogue is either heard off-
  screen while* KOOSIE *is busy, or else with* SERGE *also in the
  frame.* CAPPIE *is not seen. Although* SERGE *speaks easily
  enough to* CAPPIE, *there are undertones.*]
SERGE: Steady on the booze, Cappie.
CAPPIE: Why?
SERGE: Let's make it cosy in here.
KOOSIE: [*Looking up at the others*] Come and get it.
CAPPIE: What's on your mind, Sergeant?
SERGE: Nothing, Cap. [*He starts whistling*]
KOOSIE: You can all come and get it now.
  [*Fade.
  Later. The four men sitting around the newspaper. It is now
  quite dark.*]
SERGE: [*Pleading*] Just a small fire, Cap?
CAPPIE: No.
SERGE: He's not coming back.
CAPPIE: I said no!
SERGE: I can't see a damn thing. [*Pause*] This isn't
  cosy. [*Pause*] This isn't the way I saw it at all, quite
  frankly.
KOOSIE: Barend's got a candle.
SERGE: How about it, Barend? Be a sport man. Your
  smallest piece.
  [BAREND *takes out a stub of candle from his pocket and*

throws it on to the newspaper. KOOSIE *lights it, then holds it on one side so that the molten wax drips on to the floor. He fixes the candle firmly in this. In the light we see:* KOOSIE *and* SERGE *smiling;* BAREND *eating;* CAPPIE *is getting drunk, his self-control beginning to go. He will end up self-indulgent and loose-mouthed. From this point on a shadow of fear behind* SERGE'S *eyes whenever he speaks to* CAPPIE. *He has a premonition of what is coming and tries vainly, clumsily, to prevent it.*]

SERGE: Come on, Cap. Eat up.

CAPPIE: Looking after your old Captain, are you, Sergeant?

SERGE: That's the ticket. Eat up.

CAPPIE: [*Stroking Serge's head*] Faithful as a dog. He'd follow me into hell. Wouldn't you?

SERGE: And back... I hope. [*Tries to laugh*]
[KOOSIE *tidies up the newspaper. The dove coos.*]

KOOSIE: Listen! We forgotten the dove, Captain. [*To* BAREND] In the other room.

CAPPIE: Let's keep its fate in the balance a little longer.

SERGE: [*Eating, to* BAREND] Not so bad, hey?

CAPPIE: You're happy.

SERGE: Aren't you, Cap?

CAPPIE: If you're happy, I'm happy.

SERGE: One for all and all for one, hey!

CAPPIE: No. *You* for *me.*

SERGE: [*Trying to ignore this remark*] It's all right when there's a bunch of you... like us. What do you say, Barend? What I mean is, we're organised. The shoelaces and all. We've got a scheme. Otherwise it's hell.

CAPPIE: Start a pension fund if you like.

SERGE: If I had a place like this you know what I'd do?

CAPPIE: [*Total indifference, enunciating each word carefully*] No, we do not know what you would do if you had a place like this.

SERGE: I'd turn it into a sort of boarding house. Holiday farm style of thing. Select. No nonsense. With a games room. Ping-pong and dominoes. Could make a go of it you know. Grow my own vegetables. That's good soil out

there. Cut down costs. Even a cow. Farm butter... new-
laid eggs. What do you say, Barend?

BAREND: [*Unexpectedly*] Rhode Island Reds.

SERGE: What's that?

BAREND: They're the best for eggs.

SERGE: That a fact? [*Excessively grateful*] Rhode Island Reds.
Lovely name. I'll remember that, Barend. [*Pause*] Thanks.

BAREND: Two hundred eggs a year average.

SERGE: [*Encouraging*] Is that so!

BAREND: But you got to watch with the feeding.
Bonemeal — for the egg shells.

SERGE: [*Hanging on to the moment*] Well, I'll be...
goes to show you, hey! How come you know all about
poultry, Barend?

BAREND: We had a... hok.

SERGE: Run, fowl run.

BAREND: In the back yard.

SERGE: That must have been okay.

BAREND: Yes. It was. But I don't mind too much. You
forget. Only sometimes, you know. And my hands also.
They feel empty. It feels like I don't know what to do with
them sometimes. I worked you see... [*He stops, suddenly
aware of the three faces watching him*]

CAPPIE: Go on, Barend. This is getting nice and chummy.

SERGE: Knock if off, Cap.

CAPPIE: Serge is trying to be friendly, Barend. He's
extending a hand of friendship.

SERGE: Don't spoil everything, Cap!

CAPPIE: You'll make me jealous, Serge! Take my hand
instead. [*Pause*] Sergeant, that's an order.
[SERGE *takes* CAPPIE'S *hand and shakes it, trying to turn the
incident into a harmless joke. But when he wants to
withdraw his hand,* CAPPIE *holds on to it.*]

CAPPIE: Don't be afraid.

SERGE: I'm not afraid.

CAPPIE: I won't eat you.
[SERGE *starts whistling. With a smile,* CAPPIE *lets go of his
hand.*]

KOOSIE: Once upon a time we had pigeons. Homers and racers.

41

SERGE: And then?

KOOSIE: We had races. Beaufort West and back.

SERGE: Where's back?

KOOSIE: Cape Town.

SERGE: You can keep it.

KOOSIE: Three hundred miles one way.

SERGE: Did you gamble?

KOOSIE: You don't gamble with pigeons. It's for the sport of the thing.

SERGE: Poultry is a paying proposition. Hey, Barend? Is it true that they get lice?

KOOSIE: But sometimes they never come back. They get lost. Or hawks eat them.

SERGE: Sounds stupid to me. How could you deal with lice, Barend?

KOOSIE: Mountain View Road, Woodstock. We was number nine. Poensie was seventeen.

SERGE: Poensie?

KOOSIE: Poensie Grobbelaar. He also kept pigeons. When we going to Cape Town, Captain?

CAPPIE: Tomorrow.

SERGE: [*Worried*] You're just joking.

KOOSIE: Captain promised. My father would give us food and we could all share my room.

CAPPIE: What would your mother give us?

KOOSIE: She's dead. Sometime you must also write me another letter to my father, Captain.

CAPPIE: Tomorrow.

KOOSIE: Explaining.

CAPPIE: I'll tell him you're dead.

KOOSIE: Me?

CAPPIE: Killed in action. How's that? I'll give you a medal. Make him proud. Dear Mr...

KOOSIE: Rossouw. Jacobus Rossouw.

CAPPIE: Dear Mr Rossouw, it is my painful duty to inform you that your son...

KOOSIE: Koosie Rossouw. Aged nineteen. Brown eyes.

CAPPIE: ... is dead. Killed in action. As his commanding officer, I can say without hesitation that he died like a

42

man. He was wounded. Badly wounded. But he faced the
end without flinching.

KOOSIE: Go on.

CAPPIE: Reconnaissance patrol. Four of us. Myself,
Sergeant Atkins, Private Barend and your son with his
brown eyes. Bivouacked for the night in an old house.
Thought it was empty. But Barend... correction, Private
Barend... made us realise that we were not alone. The
enemy, Mr Rossouw... Them. A presence, something hard
and bitter, resenting us, in the shadows. We sat. Waiting.
Talked, bluffed each other with brave noises. Because, you
see, we were helpless. That is war, Mr Rossouw — time
and helplessness. And ruins. I remember Rome. Went up
there when it was over. Rome! The glory that was Greece
and the grandeur that was Rome. I stood and stared, Mr
Rossouw. Broken corners, spaces, fallen walls, pieces...
the glory, the grandeur was... and I recognised It...
Time... realised... Time. A thousand years of it in one
shell. Eternity at the end of a bayonet.
I've seen it! Smashed, and wrecked and falling! [*Pause*]
Then the guns were silent. They said we had won. Won! I
walked through a ruin... been a house I think. The dust
was settling. It was finished. Broken. That house was dead.
But such a peace, Mr Rossouw! Nothing. Silence.
Emptiness... and it was such a peace.
"It's over," they said. "We won." And then, "Go home."
Just like that. God, Home! "What?" I asked. "What must
go home? Are you blind? We're also ruins. The guns have
left our hearts in ruins! [*Pointing to* SERGE] Look at him.
We went to war!" "To defend," they said. To protect.
Justice, dignity, freedom! But *that* came back. That!
[*Indicates* SERGE] His laugh is the sound of it falling to
pieces! You want to know what the dead hate most of all
about us here tonight! His laugh! When Serge laughs they
know they're dead. And me? Once upon a time I was a
man living happily ever after. But when I came out of that
ruin... "you're going home," they said. Just like that. I
went mad. Fear! I picked up pieces — a million lives were
lying around me in pieces... I picked up pieces. But

43

nothing fits! My smile doesn't belong to my face, or my
face to my fear, or that to me... Me! Nothing fits! And
you, Barend?

SERGE: He never went to war.

CAPPIE: He's a ruin.

KOOSIE: Captain...

CAPPIE: And him.

KOOSIE: You didn't get to my medal.

CAPPIE: Medal?

KOOSIE: Koosie killed in action — in the ruins. Bravery in
in battle.

CAPPIE: What the hell! I'll give you the V.C.

SERGE: And me? [*Laughing*] I was there too.

CAPPIE: Degenerate Soldier's Order.

SERGE: And yourself?

CAPPIE: Iron Cross and the Star of David. How's that?
[BAREND *stands up and leaves the room through the
doorway to the hall.*]

CAPPIE: [*To* BAREND *as he leaves*] We promised the lady
we'd do it outside.
[*Cut from the lounge to the passage and* BAREND. *He is
standing quite still. In the distance the voices of* CAPPIE *and*
SERGE. *Though we cannot hear what they are saying the
noise becomes strident and angry.* BAREND *turns and walks
back to the lounge. The voices get clearer. The following
dialogue is off-screen.*]

SERGE: [*Emphatic*] No. No. [*There is an indistinct mumble
from* CAPPIE] I know what's coming and I say no. Just cut
it out. That's all. Why must you always spoil everything?

CAPPIE: [*A military bark*] Sergeant!

SERGE: Cut it out, Cappie!
[BAREND *reaches the doorway to the lounge. As he moves
through it, a quick change to a shot of* CAPPIE, SERGE *and*
KOOSIE. CAPPIE *is still sitting, still has his bottle.* SERGE *is
now standing. He is agitated and at first does not see*
BAREND. KOOSIE *is huddled up against a wall, fingers in his
ears, eyes tightly closed, trying not to hear what is being
said.*]

SERGE: I'm not sleeping in here if you're going to

start that. This time I mean it. [*He sees* BAREND] It's
nothing. Just... it's nothing.

CAPPIE: [*To* BAREND] What you up to? Hey? Where you
been? Visiting the little girl in her room?

SERGE: Leave him alone, Cappie.

CAPPIE: He's up to something.

SERGE: Can't we just for once go to sleep quietly?
All of us?

[KOOSIE *opens his eyes and takes his fingers away from his
ears.*]

KOOSIE: I'll clear up.

[*During the following dialogue* KOOSIE *will drift in and out
of the scene. His last exit will be through the doorway
leading to the hall and when he returns it will be with the
news that he has found the bed.*]

SERGE: This could have been cosy. Lay off the booze,
Cap. Make a resolution.

CAPPIE: I want to know what Barend's up to. Look at him!
Barend! Look us in the eye and say you're not up to
something.

SERGE: Knock it off!

CAPPIE: I'm suspicious of him.

SERGE: Go to bed.

CAPPIE: Bed! Poor old Serge. Faithful as a dog. What bed?

SERGE: All right, then the floor. Lie down and sleep it off.

CAPPIE: [*To* BAREND, *aggressively*] I'm suspicious of you.
[BAREND *sits down near what remains of the candle,
watching the flame and his hands while* CAPPIE *speaks.*]

CAPPIE: I've always been. An' you know why? You stink
of wages. And dreaming. You dream, don't you Barend?
The way you write on lavatory walls — on the sly? You
don't fool me. Nobody pulls the wool over Cappie's eyes.
What do you dream about?
[KOOSIE *returns to the lounge through the second doorway.
He goes straight to* CAPPIE.]

KOOSIE: Captain...

CAPPIE: I'll find that dream, Barend... and then I'll
piss on it.

KOOSIE: Captain, guess what?

45

CAPPIE: Roses are red, violets are blue, lilies are white
and I love you.

KOOSIE: I found a bed, Captain. A real bed.

CAPPIE: A bed.

KOOSIE: A real one. It's even got a mattress.

SERGE: Where?

KOOSIE: In the little room down there. Must I show you?
[KOOSIE *leads* CAPPIE *and* SERGE *out of the lounge, carrying
what is left of the candle on a piece of plank.* BAREND
*doesn't move. He sits alone, his back to the other three as
they leave. Shot changes to:*
The passage. KOOSIE *leading* CAPPIE *and* SERGE. *Shadows.*
Sound of the leaves and glass as they walk.]

KOOSIE: I was just looking around when I found it.
First I went to the dove and then I came down here and
found it. It's in there.
[*They reach the door. Shot changes to:*
The room. The bed. KOOSIE, CAPPIE *and* SERGE.]

KOOSIE: There. How's that, Captain?

SERGE: It's a bed all right.

KOOSIE: Definitely.

CAPPIE: How did we miss it?

SERGE: What's the odds? We've found it. Try it for size,
Cappie.

KOOSIE: Yes, you must have it Captain.

BAREND: [*Off-screen*] No! Leave it alone.
[KOOSIE, SERGE *and* CAPPIE *turn in response.* BAREND
comes through the door into the light.]

BAREND: I found it first. It's mine.

SERGE: What do you mean?

KOOSIE: I found it first.

CAPPIE: You knew about it!

BAREND: This is my room. You can have all the others.
This is mine.

CAPPIE: All the time! You knew it was here!

BAREND: Get away from it.
[BAREND *moves forward and sits on the bed. The other three
move back to the wall where they stand and watch him.*]

BAREND: I'm warning you. It's mine.

CAPPIE: So that's it.

BAREND: Get out!

CAPPIE: Home.

BAREND: Get out!

CAPPIE: Your dream is Home.

SERGE: Come, Cap.

KOOSIE: What's going on?

SERGE: Let's move.

CAPPIE: He wants a Home.

KOOSIE: Who's got a home?

BAREND: I'm warning you: Get out! This is my room.
My bed. *Mine!*

SERGE: Let's move, soldier.

[SERGE *starts pulling* CAPPIE *to the door.*]

CAPPIE: You're not one of us. You're one of them.
You're a ghost. You're dead, Barend. Dead.

[BAREND *jumps up and pushes the three out of the room, then forces the door closed. The camera stays on* BAREND. *Outside in the passage* CAPPIE *starts hammering on the door. The following dialogue is all heard off-screen through the door.*]

CAPPIE: [*Hammering*] Barend! Barend! Are you there?
[*Pause*] Listen! Barend, listen to me. [*Slowly, very carefully*] The nigger slept in the bed, Barend. Smell the room. His stink is still in the room. You've got a nigger's bed, Dutchman. [*Pause*] Barend. [*Starting to shout*] Barend!

SERGE: Come on, Cap.

KOOSIE: Let's go, Captain.

CAPPIE: We're finished with you. D'you hear. You're out.
Tomorrow you'll crawl around like a lost dog. We don't want you. [*Getting fainter*] Nobody wants you. You've had it. Barend you're ... [*Words muffled and indistinct*]
[BAREND *listens for a few more seconds, then moves back to the bed.* CAPPIE'S *voice is still heard from time to time — an indistinct jeering sound. Then silence.* BAREND *prepares for bed. From his pocket three stubs of candle, one of which he lights and places beside the bed on the floor. Rolls up his coat to use as a pillow. He is still busy when the shot changes to:*]

The lounge. KOOSIE *holding their candle. It is just about finished.*]

KOOSIE: [*Watching the candle*] Captain...

[CAPPIE *and* SERGE. SERGE *now has the bottle.* CAPPIE *is forcing him to drink.*]

SERGE: [*Desperate*] I knew it. [*He drinks*] I saw it coming.

CAPPIE: More. All of it.

SERGE: I'm still sore, Cappie. [*He drinks, the wine spilling out of his mouth*] S'true's Christ. I'm still as sore as hell.

KOOSIE: [*Off-screen*] Captain!

[CAPPIE *and* SERGE *look in* KOOSIE'S *direction. Shot changes just in time for us to see the candle guttering and then going out. Silence.*]

KOOSIE: Finished.

CAPPIE: [*To* SERGE] Bottoms up.

KOOSIE: Captain, there is still the dove.

CAPPIE: Kill it.

KOOSIE: Death sentence! I'll do it at dawn.

SERGE: Just remember it hurts. Not so rough this time.
Try and be gentle.

KOOSIE: And sentry duty, Captain? He might come again.
What's the password?

CAPPIE: Ravioli.

KOOSIE: Ravioli. You haven't got a gun for me, Captain?
Captain, you...

SERGE: [*Singing*] Roll me over, in the clover, roll me over,
lay me down and do it again.

[KOOSIE *leaves the room. Slow fade to:*
BAREND. *He is ready for bed. His shoes and socks are placed neatly on the floor beside the candle. He goes to the door, listens, then opens it and looks out. He closes it and then goes to the windows where he tries to look out through the shutters. Finally to his bed.*]

BAREND: [*Sitting on the edge of the bed*] It's late!
Tomorrow!...

[*The last word is said with emphasis, as if a statement is to follow, but then cannot be found. For a few seconds* BAREND *stares at the inscrutable surface of the word. This one word, followed by a silence which turns statement into question,*

can be repeated by BAREND *once or twice off-screen,
between this moment and the end.*
The lounge: Close-up of CAPPIE. *He is awake, curled up in a
corner. More than anything else we see his eyes — open,
alert, listening, like an animal whose only defence is to lie
quiet and hope it will not be seen. Then a shot of* SERGE,
*sprawled out on the floor, asleep. Finally a shot, the camera
again close up, of* KOOSIE. *The camera starts to move back.
We see that* KOOSIE *is holding the dove, still alive, and*
BAREND'S *stick... that he is sitting on the front verandah of
the house. The camera keeps moving back. We see the whole
house.*]

MCMA — D

The Coat

**An Acting Exercise from Serpent Players
of New Brighton**

Cast

LAVRENTI
MARIE
ANIKO
JINGI
HAEMON

Five chairs on an empty stage. The actors — three men and two women — walk on and sit down. One of the men comes forward and addresses the audience.

LAVRENTI: We are a group of actors from New Brighton. Aniko, Marie, Haemon, Jingi... [*The actors nod as they are introduced*]... and I am Lavrenti.

New Brighton. I often wonder what that name means to outsiders, like you. I am using the word in its purely descriptive sense — we live inside and you live outside. That world where your servants go at the end of the day, that ugly scab of pondokkies and squalor that spoils the approach to Port Elizabeth. If you are interested in knowing something about it we might be able to help you, because we accepted the chance to come here tonight so that we could tell you about a coat, a man's coat, which came back to New Brighton in a stranger's shopping bag. Allow me a short word of explanation.

There are many confused and even contradictory reasons for our existence as a group. The hunger for applause, boredom, conceit, desperation, even money at one stage — though we have now learnt enough to know that here in Port Elizabeth theatre is not the way you make it, but lose it. We have talked about this question of motives more times than I care to remember. But during all that talking we have discovered one thing which we all have in common, something on top of all the other reasons, or should I say at the bottom, because it hasn't been all that strong. We want to use the theatre. For what? Here it gets a bit confused again. Some of us say to understand the world we live in but we also boast a few idealists who

53

think that theatre might have something to do with changing it.

These attitudes imply something of a purpose to our work. This in turn has involved us in the life and people of New Brighton. It is the only world we know. It is real. We want our work to be real. So we study and try to understand that world — the shopkeepers and the housewives who complain about the shopkeepers; the labourers coming home tired at night and the bus conductors who don't wait for those labourers at bus stops, the tsotsis who molest the young lovers, the young lovers themselves... as one of us once put it, its problems and its pleasures.

It was in this way that we first heard and talked about the coat.

To begin with I don't think any of us believed we had anything to learn from it. That was a mistake of course — but remember we are still only beginners, still learning the first lessons and making the first mistakes.

We discovered that the coat was real. I don't mean that we didn't believe it had ever existed. We knew it had. When I say 'real' I mean we discovered that it was the cause and effect of things. We came to believe in it so strongly that we decided to use tonight to show you what had happened when we discussed and examined it.

There are certain facts; we will give you them. There are a lot of questions; we tried to find the answers. Listen and judge for yourself.

Just before we start let me answer any of you who might be asking: Why the coat? Why not the man who wore the coat? Isn't he real? Isn't a real man a better subject for an actor's exercise? Of course he is. The man would have been better, but it was the coat that came back.

One other point. We thought it might help you to follow and understand us if we had a coat something like the original to work with. Likewise the shopping bag.

Marie brought back the coat.

[LAVRENTI *sits down.* MARIE *comes forward. She carries a brown-paper shopping bag.*]

MARIE: I brought the coat back with me from Cradock, a hundred

54

and sixty miles away. I had gone to Cradock for my husband's trial. The coat isn't his. It belongs to another New Brighton man. There have been a lot of our men in the Cradock cells. The charges are mostly the same: membership of a banned organisation, distributing pamphlets, addressing a meeting and so on. They go to Robben Island afterwards. The lucky ones get three years. Most of them get five or seven.

When we got to Cradock I went straight to the Magistrate's Court. I was lucky, because all the white people were having tea so they let me see him in the courtroom. When the court is working they do not let you in. Nobody is allowed in. Only the officials. I saw my husband in the courtroom. He looked all right. He said that his case hadn't started yet. They were still busy with two other men. One of them was the owner of the coat. He was wearing it. [*She thinks very hard*] They, the two men, were sitting in the dock. There were lots of policemen and white men about, coming and going and drinking their tea. The two men sat very still. They looked about fifty. I asked my husband their names. He said that he didn't know. They were in another cell. In court they were called number one accused and number two accused. Then I went out to the cafe to buy them food. When I came back the Court was busy so I had to wait. I waited at the back near the cells. At lunchtime they came out but nothing had happened yet. They were still busy on the case of the two men. They let me see my husband. I gave him the food. We talked softly.

The Court started again at two o'clock. When I saw them at teatime the case of the two men had finished. They each got five years. My husband's case then started but when he came out at five o'clock it wasn't finished. I went around to the cells to say goodbye because I had to go home. I could only get one day off from my work.

[MARIE *speaks slowly now, concentrating hard on giving every detail, trying to be as clear and factual as possible.*] While I was talking to him the two men came past. The one with the coat came up to me quickly and asked me to see his wife and children. He gave me the address. He asked me to tell them what had happened to him. Then he took off his coat and said I must give it to his wife. "Tell her to use it," he said. "Tell them I will come back."

I said goodbye to them. Outside I folded up the coat and put it in the shopping bag in which I had brought my husband's clean clothes. I brought it back with me to New Brighton.

On the way back — I think it was near Cookhouse — the van with the prisoners passed us. It was going very fast. One man was looking out through the back window. I think it was him, the one who gave me the coat.

I went to the address the next day. It was in Mnqandi Street. I knocked on the door and an old woman opened it. She was alone. It was the wife. I told her why I had come and gave her the coat. In front of me she went through all the pockets. All she found was a little piece of brown paper with some powder inside. She told me she had got it from a witchdoctor to keep the sentence small. She said it had worked, because she had heard about other men who had got twenty years.

I gave her the message from her husband — that she must use the coat and wait for him — then said goodbye and left.

LAVRENTI: [*Coming forward*] What sort of coat was it?

MARIE: Oh, just an old coat. A man's sportscoat.

LAVRENTI: Torn?

MARIE: I don't think it was torn. It might have had patches, but it wasn't torn.

LAVRENTI: So it was worth something.

MARIE: Certainly. One rand, one rand fifty. Something like that.

LAVRENTI: [*To the audience*] Those were our facts. The first thing we did was to improvise the little scene where the coat was handed over. We wanted to see it, that moment, when it passed from the hands of a stranger to the wife, because that is when the coat starts to live again, where it comes back into our lives.

Aniko will take the part of the wife.

So then, here it is: The Scene In Which The Wife Gets

Back Her Husband's Coat.

[LAVRENTI *sits down,* ANIKO *joins* MARIE.]

MARIE: Hello Mama.

ANIKO: Hello my child.

MARIE: How are you Mama?

ANIKO: I am all right my child. I am all right. How are you?

MARIE: Carrying on Mama. Trying to carry on. These are hard times.

ANIKO: Yes, these are hard times, but we must carry on. There is nothing else for people like us to do.

MARIE: I came to see you Mama because your husband asked me. I saw him yesterday at Cradock. My husband is also one of those up there.

ANIKO: Yes.

MARIE: Your husband got five years Mama.

ANIKO: Yes.

MARIE: He asked me to tell you and to say he was all right.

ANIKO: Five years.

MARIE: He gave me his coat Mama and told me to give it to you. He said you must use it, and wait for him. [MARIE *takes out the coat*] Here it is.

ANIKO: Yes, that's his coat. [*She takes it*] He'll be cold now, without it.

MARIE: They wouldn't have let him keep it. They take everything away and give you prison clothes.

ANIKO: Short trousers.

MARIE: And a shirt.

ANIKO: He's an old man for short trousers. [*She examines the coat*] It's a good coat.

MARIE: There is still a lot of use in it Mama. Maybe it will fit one of your sons.

ANIKO: Is there anything in the pockets?

MARIE: I didn't look Mama. I bring it just as he gave it to me.

ANIKO: [*Going through the pockets*] He got it last year. From a baas at his work. He used to do some jobs for him in the garden on Saturdays. One day he gave him this coat. What did he look like, my child, yesterday?

MARIE: He looked all right Mama. They say the food isn't too bad.

ANIKO: Where is he now?

MARIE: I think here in Port Elizabeth. At the Rooi Hell. The van with the prisoners passed me on the road when I was coming back. They will write and tell you where they are going to take him. Some of them go to Robben Island.

[ANIKO *finds a little twist of brown paper in one of the pockets.*]

ANIKO: Ja, he kept it.

MARIE: What Mama?

ANIKO: They told me to get some medicine to keep the number of years of his sentence small. I gave it to him when he was here at the Rooi Hell. It worked. It was strong. There are families in this street who won't see their men for ten years.

I will wait for him. I will keep this coat for him.

[MARIE *hesitates, on the verge of saying something, but changes her mind.*]

MARIE: Goodbye Mama.

ANIKO: Goodbye and God bless you my child.

[MARIE *walks back to her chair.*]

LAVRENTI: You hesitated there, as if you wanted to say something.

MARIE: Yes, I know. I wanted to tell her it was silly to keep the coat all that time if she could use it. Five years is long.

LAVRENTI: Why didn't you?

MARIE: I don't know. I felt sorry for her.

LAVRENTI: [*To* ANIKO *who is still by herself*] So now the coat is with the old woman. What did you, as the wife, feel when you got it back?

ANIKO: I'm not sure. I wasn't really in it yet you know, in the part.

LAVRENTI: What do you think she felt? Was she sad, or...

JINGI: Of course she was sad. She's lost her husband for five years.

HAEMON: But remember she said she thought he might have got longer. She must have also been a little bit relieved.

ANIKO: Can I work it out? Give me a chair. [LAVRENTI *moves forward* ANIKO'S *chair.*] The Scene Where The Old Woman Is Alone With The Coat.

When Marie left she hung it up... Ja!... and then she said a prayer.

Thanks God it's all over. After waiting for so long, now I

58

know I only have to wait for five years. It could have been longer. God please give me strength to wait, and look after him in gaol. Thanks God.

Ja, then she goes on with her housework. I am alone in the house. I look at the coat. I think about the man. His name is Temba. Temba's coat.

[ANIKO *has moved slowly into the character of the old woman.*] Ja Temba. Five years. One two three four five years. It's easy to count it. But how long is five years? It's a long time in a man's life. You will be older when you come back to Mnqandi Street. We will be older. Our daughter is ten. She will be fifteen. Our son is sixteen. He will be a man. Ja Temba. He must be a man before his time.

I must look for work now. Do washing for a white Madam. Joyce next door will help me to find work. Five years! A lot of things can happen. Lots of things do happen. Six months ago you were still walking down Mnqandi Street in the early morning with the other men to work. At night you came back. And now?

Where are you now? Cradock. Robben Island. Where is Robben Island? Far away I think.

And your coat. Temba's coat. You said you will come back. You said we must wait. Will they let you come back Temba? When your five years is past will they open the gates and let you out?

Ai! The white people. What is it all about? What is the matter with them? They have got everything. And now they also take our men away.

You will look older when you come back to us. What did you look like the last time I saw you? When was the last time I saw you? In gaol. At the Rooi Hell.

I stood with food and waited outside the big doors with the other women. We stood a long time. Then they opened the door and let us in . . . one by one. You were still wearing this coat. You asked about the children. You said you were all right.

[*Pause. She thinks hard.*] It's hard to remember what you looked like. Sometimes here in the house, at night, you looked tired. We were getting old, Temba.

And now? We must wait. We must live without you for five years. It will be hard. But I can do washing. Joyce must help me find a white Madam with washing...

[ANIKO *breaks off with a weary gesture and turns to the other actors. She speaks as herself.*] Tired fellows. I think she feels tired. Looking for washing is hell man. Those old women walk Boetie. And all that waiting there at the gaol! Ai, no!

LAVRENTI: So?

ANIKO: So you asked me what I think the old girl feels and I'm saying she feels *moeg*.

JINGI: And sad.

ANIKO: I felt tired.

MARIE: But don't you think she asked too many questions? Everything was a question.

ANIKO: That's what made me tired. Every time I thought something, there was a question. Questions without answers is hell man.

LAVRENTI: Let's get back to the coat. His message was: "Tell her to use it." Let's see it being used. How does she use it? Go on, use it.

[*Pause.* ANIKO *thinks.*]

ANIKO: It's night time and cold. Raining maybe. We're all asleep. Then I hear one of the children on the floor — the girl — shivering. I get up and take her father's coat and put it on her like a blanket.

JINGI: Were they as poor as that? No beds, no blankets?

MARIE: No, I don't think they were so poor.

JINGI: Exactly! Mnqandi Street is a good address.

LAVRENTI: Hang on. That's no criticism. Aniko can't be limited to facts which she doesn't know. She was giving us *her* old woman, and there are enough old women and their children sleeping on the floor to make that possible.

ANIKO: What do you mean possible? It *happens* man.

HAEMON: I've got a better idea for using the coat. Can we try it.

LAVRENTI: Go ahead.

[HAEMON *joins* ANIKO *taking his chair with him.*]

HAEMON: I am the son at school. My father is now in gaol serving

60

his five years. My mother is struggling to support us. I can see she is worried. So I am going to ask her to let me leave school and get a job.

MARIE: How does the coat come into it?

HAEMON: I'm coming to that. I've heard about a job and I want to go and apply. But my own coat is torn. You must be smart to get a job. So I am going to ask her to lend me my father's coat.

ANIKO: We are in the house?

HAEMON: Yes. It's supper time. I've got my samp and beans and I'm sitting next to the stove where it's warm. You're sitting at the table. I can see you are worried.

LAVRENTI: Right. So then. The Scene Where The Son Borrows The Father's Coat To Look For A Job.

[ANIKO *and* HAEMON *take up positions. He eats in silence for a few seconds and watches his mother. Then he gets up and moves his chair beside her.*]

HAEMON: You look worried tonight, Mama.

ANIKO: I am just thinking, my boy.

HAEMON: Have we got this week's rent, Mama?

ANIKO: Yes. I think we will have it.

HAEMON: And food, Mama?

ANIKO: What are you worrying about these things for! Worry about your lessons at school. I haven't let you go hungry yet.

HAEMON: But I must worry, Mama. You are alone. I am my father's son.

ANIKO: He will be back with us one day.

HAEMON: We still have a long time to wait.

ANIKO: Yes.

HAEMON: We are struggling, Mama.

ANIKO: So are a lot of other people in New Brighton.

HAEMON: Yes, but you are alone. They have got uncles, and families... you are alone.

ANIKO: My sister sent me two rand last week from East London.

HAEMON: Will she send you two rand again this week, and next week...

ANIKO: No. She can't. She is poor. But why are you going on like this? I know all these things. But I am trying my best.

61

HAEMON: I want to get a job, Mama. I want to leave school and get a job.

ANIKO: No.

HAEMON: Please, Mama...

ANIKO: No!

HAEMON: Please just listen to me, Mama.

ANIKO: No! You go to school. You learn. If your father had gone to school maybe he wouldn't be where he is now. You learn to read and write.

HAEMON: I can already read and write, Mama.

ANIKO: Then learn more. Learn all you can and keep yourself out of gaol. This world is too clever now for old people like your father and me, but you can learn about it.

HAEMON: Mama...

ANIKO: I said no! Have you lost your manners that you do not listen to a big person any more?

HAEMON: Mama, I am my father's son. I am your son. Just listen to me once.

   We need money, Mama. You said yourself that we must see that we are here when Father comes back. But how can we stay here if we don't pay the rent? How can we be alive if we don't eat? How can we eat without money? Please, Mama! Listen to me. If I get a job it will be easier. I won't stop learning. I will go to night school. I can still write my exams.

ANIKO: The last time I saw your Father in gaol he asked me how you were getting on at school. He said to me: "He must learn. The white man's world is a strange one. Tell him to be clever."

HAEMON: I can do all that at night school, Mama. Other boys do it. They work during the day and study at night. I will do what my Father wants. But I also want to be here when he comes back.

ANIKO: You don't even know if you can get a job.

HAEMON: I can, Mama. George Ngxokolo told me about one. It's at the same place where he works. One of the white Madams called him and said he must look for a good boy for them in New Brighton.

ANIKO: How much is the pay?

HAEMON: Five rands a week.

ANIKO: That will help.

HAEMON: Can I go tomorrow and see them?

ANIKO: Your Father will not forgive me.

HAEMON: Father will understand, Mama. When I tell him how you struggled and all our troubles, he will understand.

ANIKO: What time must you be at this place?

HAEMON: Early, Mama. George said I must be there early to show them I will always be early.

ANIKO: I will give you bus fare.

HAEMON: George also said I must look smart.

ANIKO: Your other shirt is clean.

HAEMON: But my jacket is so old, Mama.

ANIKO: It's all we've got.

HAEMON: [*Hesitantly*] Couldn't I borrow father's jacket? Just to get the job! I'll look after it. It will help me get the job.

ANIKO: Yes, you can borrow it.

HAEMON: [*Turning to the other actors*] That's all.

LAVRENTI: [*To* HAEMON] Put on the coat.

[HAEMON *puts it on.*]

JINGI: It fits.

LAVRENTI: I like this. We've got the coat being worn, being used.

JINGI: I've got reservations about the scene though.

MARIE: I thought it was right. What was wrong with it?

JINGI: I think Haemon was too advanced for his age.

HAEMON: How?

JINGI: How old were you supposed to be?

HAEMON: Sixteen years.

JINGI: And you want to tell me that a sixteen-year-old boy will discuss things with his mother like that? Will worry and care like that?

MARIE: Yes.

JINGI: Never.

ANIKO: Boet Jingi! I know of a case in our street, man, just like that. There are older boys in the family but they do nothing. It's the young one who helps his mother. He sells newspapers at night, during weekends he gets garden jobs in Newton Park. In fact I think he is younger than fifteen.

HAEMON: Yes, you get them.

HAEMON: So what must we do about those that do? Pretend they don't exist?

JINGI: If we are concerned with New Brighton, and understanding it...

HAEMON: But loyalty to your parents, understanding, sympathy, self-sacrifice ... these are also part of New Brighton. Aren't they?

JINGI: Look Haemon, I challenge you ...

HAEMON: He's not answering my question. Is New Brighton all bad? Don't people, the young people, have any good points?

LAVRENTI: Answer his question.

JINGI: Yes, they do. A few of them.

HAEMON: Well I think we must understand them just as much as the others. Maybe they are the most important of all.

MARIE: Hear, hear!

HAEMON: Why concern ourselves with New Brighton at all if there is nothing good to say about it?
I think that woman's son, the son who stands by his mother and tries to help, is more important than ten of the other kind. You can show the other kind if you want to. I showed you the son who I believed in.

LAVRENTI: Let's go back to the improvisation. I wonder whether the wife would have given the coat away so easily, even to her son.

JINGI: What percentage?

HAEMON: I don't know.

JINGI: Exactly.

HAEMON: But you get them.

JINGI: They're a very small minority, my friend.

HAEMON: So what?

JINGI: So what are we trying to do? Aren't we trying to find out something about New Brighton?

LAVRENTI: Yes, we are.

JINGI: Then let's concern ourselves with the majority. And I'm saying that the majority of young boys and girls, and men and women for that matter, don't give a damn about what is going on, not even in their own homes. They don't help their mothers the way Haemon showed us.

JINGI: Same here.

ANIKO: You fellows better listen better next time. I didn't give it away. I lent it to him.

HAEMON: Ewè, Mama.

LAVRENTI: All right, it's not a criticism. Let's make it a question. Would the wife give away the coat?

MARIE: No.

LAVRENTI: Even if she was pressed? Aniko?

ANIKO: What do you mean pressed? Hard-up?

LAVRENTI: Yes.

ANIKO: Ai Boet Lavrenti! You want to see this old woman in trouble hey!

LAVRENTI: Well, what do you think?

ANIKO: Maybe. Maybe no. I don't know.

JINGI: Suppose one of your children is sick.

ANIKO: Then I'll buy medicine.

JINGI: But you haven't any money. You're broke.

LAVRENTI: Hang on. Give her the coat. [HAEMON *takes off the coat and gives it to* ANIKO. *He stands a little to one side but doesn't sit.*] Okay Jingi.

JINGI: [*To* ANIKO] One of your children is sick. The ten-year-old girl. The doctor has told you she must get some certain kind of medicine straight away. But you're broke. It's the end of the week so Haemon hasn't got his pay yet. But you've got the coat. You could sell it. Marie told us it was worth about one rand, one rand fifty. That will be enough for medicine with enough left over for a bucket of entrails. The child is sick. She needs medicine and good food. What do you say? The child is crying man! Listen to her! There in the other room, crying Mama! Mama! Here is one rand fifty. Give me the coat and it's yours.

ANIKO: No man. Maybe there is something else. I've got two pots. Take one.

JINGI: One old pot? What's that worth? Two bob! And anyway it's got a hole in it and no lid . . .

ANIKO: There must be something else! My zinc bath . . . No. I need it for the washing.

JINGI: What are you worrying about? What's your problem? The coat hangs there useless in the wardrobe. Nobody wears it.

65

Nobody is going to be cold. You could save up and buy him a much better one for when he comes back. Times will change. He didn't say you must keep it for him. He said: "Use it. Tell her to use it." Those were his words. Well now his daughter is sick. There in the other room. Wouldn't he be the first one to tell you to sell it? Here it is in my hand. One rand fifty. Give me the coat and it's yours. What about it?

[ANIKO *looks at the outstretched, clenched fist of* JINGI. *She is about to hand over the coat when* HAEMON *jumps forward.*]

HAEMON: No Mama! I'll borrow from my baas at work. He will lend it to me.

ANIKO: [*Clutching the coat to herself and turning away from* JINGI] Thank you my son.

[MARIE *claps her hands and laughs.* LAVRENTI *smiles.* JINGI *drops his hand with a hopeless gesture to the other actors returns to his seat.* LAVRENTI *gets up.*]

LAVRENTI: [*To* HAEMON] You cheated.

JINGI: Ja! That was a sure case of interference.

HAEMON: She is my mother. It was my father's coat.

LAVRENTI: But we wanted her on the spot man.

HAEMON: Then you shouldn't have told me to try on the coat.

LAVRENTI: What difference did that make?

HAEMON: I thought about my father.

LAVRENTI: You are complicating matters with your loyalty.

HAEMON: That's right.

LAVRENTI: [*Smiling*] Okay, okay, we get you. But let's try again. Because I think it's a good question. Would she ever sell the coat? Come on, let's try and work out a situation in which she is really in a tight corner and the only way out is to sell the coat. Jingi had a good try with that idea of the sick child but there were too many loopholes.

JINGI: What about hunger? Starvation? Food. A hungry person will do anything for food.

MARIE: Her neighbours wouldn't let her starve. We've heard about this woman Joyce... she wouldn't let this old woman starve.

JINGI: What? There are plenty of families that go to sleep at night

66

with only a mug of hot water in their bellies and their neighbours don't give a damn.

LAVRENTI: Hold it. Hold it. Let's not get back to that argument.

MARIE: What about funeral expenses? Suppose the little girl had died from her illness and the old woman needed money for funeral expenses. You know how fussy our people are about burials and all that.

ANIKO: No man. Sis Marie! Jesus! I'll commit suicide. That's my answer. My husband is in gaol, now my daughter dies! I don't want to live any more.

What's the matter with you people? Why don't you just get a big lorry to knock her down and kill her and get it over with?

LAVRENTI: We want her alive. She's no good to us dead.

ANIKO: Then have pity on her.

LAVRENTI: There's not much of that in life, sister. But anyway you're right, let's not exaggerate the circumstances. Just a nice straightforward case of destitution. Hardly enough money for one meal, no money for clothes or ... Come on!

JINGI: Rent.

LAVRENTI: Ja, rent! That's a thought. There's a nice typical New Brighton predicament. How about it?

JINGI: She's fallen two months behind in her rent. The Headman has brought around a final notice. If she doesn't pay up straight away she gets out. We could have a scene where she sits and thinks about the final notice.

ANIKO: I can't read.

MARIE: So you call in Joyce from next door. Maybe she can. You can discuss things with her.

LAVRENTI: And then?

JINGI: Then she goes to the Administration Office to plead with the Headman to give her a week to find some money. He tells her that she must pay something straight away. I've got it! He's a member of one of those money-lending societies that get rich on the poor people ... so he sends her along to his society to sell her coat.

LAVRENTI: We've got it. Okay Aniko? Marie will be your neighbour, Jingi will be the Headman at the Administration Offices. Then you go to borrow money from the Society and Marie will be that woman as well.

ANIKO: What about Haemon? I want Haemon. He helps me.

HAEMON: Yes, you must reckon with the two of us now.

LAVRENTI: We want her alone.

HAEMON: That's not fair.

LAVRENTI: Fair doesn't come into it. We're black.

HAEMON: But she *has* got a son.

LAVRENTI: Look man, this is an experiment... a theatre laboratory. We are allowed to isolate a factor for examination. So let us assume that for some reason or other you cannot interfere in this one. Okay?

HAEMON: Not even to give her moral support?

LAVRENTI: All right, if you want to. That's useless enough. Right. The Scene Where The Wife Is Faced With Selling Her Husband's Coat To Pay Her Rent.

[LAVRENTI *sits down.* HAEMON *sits down by himself to one side.* ANIKO *is alone.*]

ANIKO: Sis Joyce! Sis Joyce!

MARIE: [*Seated*] What is it?

ANIKO: Come here please, Sis Joyce!

MARIE: [*Joining* ANIKO] What is wrong?

ANIKO: Hai Sis Joyce! Is it true? Do they want to throw me out of my house? The Headman brought me this paper. Is it true?

MARIE: Tula Sissy. Tula. Let me read it. [*Reading*] That unless the arrears of twenty-four rand are paid immediately you will be evicted from the house... Hey hey hey! Haven't you been paying your rent?

ANIKO: These last four months have been terrible, Sis Joyce. Every week I said this week I will pay the rent, even if I go hungry. But when the children come home and they are hungry but I see they are too frightened to ask if there is any food... what must a mother do? Then the little girl was sick, John lost his job... Is it true that they want to throw me out? Does the paper say so?

MARIE: Yes, if you don't pay them what you owe.

ANIKO: What must I do?

MARIE: Go to the Headman at the Office. Speak to him Sissy. Ask him to speak with the Superintendent. Plead with him. Sis Nkonyeni got this paper one time and she went there and

68

spoke to them and they gave her more time to find the money.

ANIKO: I will go straight away.

[MARIE *sits down.*] It took me thirty minutes to get to the Administration Offices. One long walk, straight, straight down from Mnqandi Street. It's a rough road. I was in a hurry. I tripped and fell, I got up and carried on. Past the White Location until I came to the offices.

There are people in the yard, sitting and waiting. It is a hot day. There is no shade. I sat with them and waited. The ones who were before you go in. They look worried. When they come out they still look worried. Some of them get a piece of paper inside. They walk away looking at it. Then your turn comes.

[JINGI *moves forward his chair, sits down, and pretends to write.* ANIKO *moves up to him, he looks up at her and goes on writing. He keeps her waiting a long time.*]

JINGI: Have you got the money?

Hey! I'm speaking to you. Have you got the money? Twenty-four rand.

ANIKO: No . . .

JINGI: Then what are you wasting my time for? Go and find the money.

ANIKO: Please Sibonda . . . please give me till the end of this month. My son is looking for a job . . . I know he will find one, he is a good boy. I am going to do washing. I will have some money at the end of the month.

JINGI: This rent must be paid no later than the date shown on your notice.

ANIKO: Ag sies tog, my father! Can't you please speak to the Superintendent for me? I can't speak his language.

JINGI: I can't bother him! He's a busy man. Do you think he's got time to sit around and listen to sad stories? Pay your rent or get out of the house.

ANIKO: Won't you take me to him, let me speak to him?

JINGI: You want me to lose my job?

ANIKO: [*Turning to leave*] Oh my God, what am I going to do now?

JINGI: Anyway, where's your husband?

ANIKO: In gaol for five years. On Robben Island.

JINGI: Haven't you got anybody to help you raise the money?

ANIKO: No.

JINGI: Not even two rand?

ANIKO: Two rand? I thought the paper said twenty-four.

JINGI: I know what the paper said! But if you could put down two rand I might be able to get you another week.

ANIKO: Two rand?

JINGI: Yes, two rand. Are you deaf?

ANIKO: I haven't got two rand.

JINGI: Why don't you borrow from the societies?

ANIKO: I don't know any of them.

JINGI: Look, I'll help you. There is a society at Number Five Nikwe Street... June Molefe... tell her I sent you. She will lend you money if you have something to put down as security... your sewing machine, or kitchen chairs...

ANIKO: I don't have those.

JINGI: You must have something.

ANIKO: A man's coat.

JINGI: That will do, if it's still in good condition.

ANIKO: How much is the interest?

JINGI: Twenty-five cents a week on every two rand.

ANIKO: You will give me another week if I pay two rand?

JINGI: Yes, but don't say I said so.

ANIKO: I will go and see the June.

JINGI: I will keep this order until you come back.

[ANIKO *moves away.* JINGI *rejoins the other actors.*]

ANIKO: I walked back all the way to Mnqandi Street to fetch the coat. It was a long walk. I was tired. I cried. The streets of New Brighton made me cry. A child saw I was crying and asked me why. He had two oranges. Buy an orange Mama he said. One cent each. I didn't have words for him. I didn't have words for myself. I just walked.

At the house I drank a glass of water, took the coat and started to walk to Nikwe Street. I passed Avenue A, then the Roman Church but I didn't look at it. Then into Pendla Road and up into Jolobe Road, past the Newell High School. But I didn't see anything. All I knew was that the roads are full of stones.

I reached number five Nikwe Street. I knocked on the

70

door... [MARIE *moves forward*]... a woman opened it. I told her my business. She took the coat... [MARIE *takes the coat and examines it*]... and said she would lend me two rand. She gave me the coat to hold, went away and came back with the money.

MARIE: [*Holding out her hand*] Two rand Mama. [ANIKO *holds the coat. She doesn't move*] Two rand for the coat Mama. [*Still* ANIKO *doesn't move*] Are you all right Mama?

ANIKO: [*Turning to the other actors who are watching her expectantly*] Don't just sit there and pity her.

LAVRENTI: What else can we do?

ANIKO: But a man wore this coat! [*Pause*] You think it's easy? Just hand it over and take the money! This is all that's left of him. It came back to New Brighton empty, but there was a man in it once... my husband, my children's father.

LAVRENTI: What are you trying to tell us? We know the facts.

ANIKO: No you don't. There are other facts. Life isn't just eating samp and beans, with meat once a week, or washing the white man's underpants and sleeping in Council houses. We are a nation with men, and one of them wore this coat. Can I not struggle a little for him? When he comes back can I not say: "Yes, it was hard for us as well. But we waited. We had faith. Here is your coat my husband. We kept it for you."

LAVRENTI: That's moving, Aniko... but how much of that is you, how much the wife? We're not interested in what you would *like* to see happen, but in what *does* happen.
Where is that husband going to come back to if you leave the house? And if you do leave it you know they'll most probably endorse you out and back into the Reserves.
How will you live there? Where will your son find work or carry on with his studies?

ANIKO: [*After a pause*] Then I must sell it?

LAVRENTI: Work it out. Do you want that house for another week?

ANIKO: Yes.

JINGI: Won't another week give you and your son a chance to raise the money for your back rent?

ANIKO: Yes.

71

LAVRENTI: Don't you want to be in that house, waiting, when your husband comes back?

ANIKO: Yes.

LAVRENTI: What do you think that coat is going to look like in five years' time? All you'll have left to give him is a moth-eaten, useless old rag.

ANIKO: [*Wearily*] Yes yes yes ... *yes*, to all your questions, yes to to all my feelings, my worries, yes to my children, yes to you my husband.

LAVRENTI: Go back to June Molefe at Number Five Nikwe Street.
[ANIKO *turns and moves back to* MARIE. MARIE *holds out her hand again.*]

MARIE: Two rand Mama. Two rand for the coat.
[ANIKO *hands over the coat and takes the money.*]

LAVRENTI: Okay.
[*The actors sit around in their chairs.*]

JINGI: One thought struck me, isn't there some organisation that has been paying the rents of these wives who have their husbands on Robben Island?

MARIE: It's been banned.

JINGI: Yes, but the churches have taken over, haven't they?

LAVRENTI: It would still be easy for them to miss one woman. There's over a thousand families in New Brighton with husbands and fathers on the Island.

ANIKO: You fellows sure gave that old woman a workout. First this, then that ...

HAEMON: Wasn't there a man in the Bible who suffered a series of calamities?

JINGI: Job. He was tested by God.

LAVRENTI: How about it Aniko? You think God was testing the old girl?

ANIKO: We aren't prophets man, we're people.

HAEMON: I wonder now if we spent too much time on the coat. We didn't say anything about the man. From the moment I put on that coat I started to think about my father. And what about Cradock?

LAVRENTI: At the start we said that our concern was with New Brighton.

HAEMON: Cradock has become a part of New Brighton.

LAVRENTI: That's interesting geography.

HAEMON: I think we should have said something about Cradock and that courtroom.

JINGI: You can. I don't know anything about it.

HAEMON: We didn't know anything about the coat, but we guessed.

LAVRENTI: [*Correcting him*] We had facts and we investigated.

HAEMON: There are facts about Cradock. We could do the same thing there. The real drama is surely the man who wore the coat.

MARIE: The wives wait. That is also drama.

LAVRENTI: We didn't do too badly. Because it was just a coat, we struck a good balance between reason and emotion. Our boredom kept us objective.

HAEMON: Are you saying that we must be bored with these things before we can understand them, or do anything about them?

LAVRENTI: Let's take that up next time.

[*The actors leave the stage.*]

Mille Miglia

A Play for Television

Cast

STIRLING MOSS
DENIS JENKINSON
ALFRED NEUBAUER
HUGO
MECHANICS
PRIEST
WAITER
EXTRAS

1. THE INTERIOR OF A GARAGE. A WEEK BEFORE THE RACE
(I.E. APRIL 23RD, 1955). DAY
*Cluttered work benches and equipment. Standing around the
sides are a number of cars. There is a mechanic in the office at
the back. In the centre of the floor, a Mercedes Benz 300 SLR.*
NEUBAUER *and* HUGO *are seen, and* JENKINSON *who turns to*
MOSS.

2. LATER THE SAME DAY
MOSS *and* JENKINSON *are in the cockpit,* MOSS *behind the wheel.
They are wearing their ordinary clothes. Suddenly and
simultaneously the lights are on and blinking and the horn
sounding very loudly.* JENKINSON *presses a little button attached
to the grab-rail on his right. Lights and horn again.* MOSS
switches on the engine, and it roars into life. Switches off.
NEUBAUER: He was only our number four — a reserve! — just in
   case one of the other three ran into trouble and needed a
   second car.
MOSS: [*Amused*] Number four...
JENKINSON: Brauchitsch... Caracciolo... and Lang.
NEUBAUER: Yes, Brauchitsch, Caracciolo and Lang. The first
   time around I couldn't believe my eyes. Our cars were in
   the first four places. Brauchitsch was leading, driving like
   a madman, Seaman second. They came into the pits on the
   sixteenth lap, Brauchitsch for fuel and tyres, Seaman just
   for fuel. There you have the difference. Then it happened.
   Brauchitsch was impatient... I can still see it so clearly...
   banging on the side of his car, "Schnell! Schnell!" The pit
   crew was nervous. The mechanic with the petrol fumbled
   and in a second — five gallons all over the car! Then

77

whoosh! Flames! At the other pit Seaman was ready to go. Lindemaier's overalls were in flames, but he worked the starter for him and a second later your countryman was back in the race. Three hours later he crossed the finish line first.

JENKINSON: Lang second.

NEUBAUER: I have only kissed a few drivers, Stirling, but your countryman was one of them.

[*They move to a map of Italy hanging on the wall. The route of the Mille Miglia has been traced out in red.*]

MOSS: It's a long drive to get back where you started from.

NEUBAUER: We'll have a few trial runs on the autostrada tomorrow — you and Fangio in the morning, Kling and Hermann in the afternoon. While Hugo shows you all over the car. After that, the inspection on Friday, and let's hope we're lucky in the draw for starting times.

JENKINSON: Behind the Ferraris.

MOSS: Yes. I'd like to do the chasing.

JENKINSON: No changes in their team?

NEUBAUER: No. Maglioli, Costellotti, Marzotto and Taruffi.

MOSS: It's going to be quite a race.

NEUBAUER: Ferrari's determined to make it another Italian victory, but we have four excellent drivers, excellent cars, excellent mechanics, and the best team manager in the world. [*The map*] So, Mille Miglia, 1955. An Englishman hasn't won it yet.

MOSS: [*Smiling*] Let's drink that toast.

[*They leave, on their way through the garage stopping to have another look at the car, where the mechanics are still at work.*]

MOSS: [*Close up*] Safe as a baby's cradle when they're standing still.

3. THE GARAGE. DAY. APRIL 24TH

MOSS *and* JENKINSON *in overalls in the car,* NEUBAUER *and mechanics to one side.* NEUBAUER *has a stopwatch.*

NEUBAUER: [*Starting the watch*] Go!

[MOSS *and* JENKINSON *jump out of the car and then quickly and methodically change one of the tyres. Each knows*]

exactly what he must do. Ad lib shooting of boot of car, then jack, then boot, front wheel, close-ups.
When they are finished, they jump back into the car.
NEUBAUER *stops the watch. A murmur of appreciation from the mechanics.*]

NEUBAUER: One minute and twenty-five seconds.

[*The mechanics applaud.*]

NEUBAUER: Yes. A good performance.

MOSS: Not bad for a journalist.

[JENKINSON *laughs.*]

NEUBAUER: Hugo! [*Leaving*]

[MOSS *and* JENKINSON *join* HUGO *at the bonnet.* JENKINSON *has a clipboard and makes notes as* HUGO *talks. To begin with, he demonstrates the mechanism that opens the bonnet. Both* MOSS *and* JENKINSON *try.*]

HUGO: Now, firing order of spark plugs. One, two, three, four, five, six, seven and eight. [*Tapping each one with a screwdriver*] The spares, together with the spanner, are under the driver's seat. Here. [*He goes round and shows them*] Wiring. Battery... coil... distributor... [*He launches into an explanation of the wiring.*]

4. LATER
HUGO *is still talking to an attentive* MOSS *and* JENKINSON, *the latter still making notes.*

HUGO: It is not necessary to loosen these. And remember, even after only a few minutes of driving it will be too hot to touch. Keep your gloves on. The spare is with the windscreen wipers...

JENKINSON: [*Checking back*] Under the passenger seat.

HUGO: Under the passenger seat. Now the fuel injection system. [*Again indicating the appropriate parts, he begins to explain this aspect of the Mercedes 300 SLR.*]

5. THE INTERIOR OF A LOUNGE IN BRESCIA. DAY
Flashback to several months earlier — February. First discussions. MOSS, JENKINSON *and* NEUBAUER *are sitting around a table which is cluttered with maps, notebooks, papers, etc.*

MOSS: Call it what you like — applied intelligence — but it's the only way a non-Italian can ever hope to win the Mille Miglia. It's how Bannister got to the four-minute mile. Knowing the length of his stride to a millimetre, the weight of his shoes to the fraction of an ounce, and then pacing himself so that he crossed the finish line totally exhausted. That's how I'm going to drive this time, and that's where Denis comes in.

JENKINSON: I've sorted out my notes from the four other tries in the Jags, together with his effort last year with Abecassis. About two hundred and fifty miles down on paper.

NEUBAUER: Leaving seven hundred and fifty.

MOSS: Exactly.

JENKINSON: And even these [*The notes*] are not anywhere near accurate enough for our plan. [*Reading*] . . . fifteen kilometres outside Pescara, S-bend, then sharp left-hander, bad surface in rain . . . That's all!

MOSS: [*Taut, controlled excitement*] Do you understand, Alfred? We've got to know what that corner's limit is, in the SLR, driving nine-tenths . . .

JENKINSON: Under all conditions . . . rain, sunshine.

MOSS: Our practice runs are going to tell us what I can do there and along every other inch of that thousand miles. That S-bend and the corner . . . let's imagine it's full throttle in third gear, then down to second as we go into the corner . . . suppose there's a nice straight afterwards . . .

JENKINSON: [*His notes*] . . . there is.

MOSS: So it's flat out in top. That's our interpretation, let's say under ideal conditions. There's a different one if it's raining and so on. Denis gets all of that down on paper, including the landmarks or kilometre stones he's going to navigate by. When we come to it, he'll tell me . . . no, he signals —

NEUBAUER: Signals?

MOSS: We're going to work out a set of hand signals. He signals S-bend swinging left-right full throttle in third, sharp left-hander, change down to second and after that, because it's a nice day and we're racing, flat out in top! Every detail of those roads, the corners — blind brows, bridges, the long straights where I can really open up and go...

JENKINSON: Places where we might break the car, like bumpy
railway crossings, sudden dips, bad surfaces...

MOSS: Tramlines! They're hell just outside Florence, remember.
[JENKINSON *makes a note*] Taruffi doesn't have to
remember any of that any more. He knows the route
blindfold. He's raced the Miglia twelve times already and
grew up on those roads. The same goes for the others —
Signolfi, Costellotti, Maglioli. Well, this time I won't be
wasting time trying to remember what comes next, and
then slowing down because I can't. I'll drive, and Denis
will give it to me as fast as I can drive.

NEUBAUER: In the SLR 300 that could mean one hundred and
eighty miles an hour. You will have to trust each other.

MOSS: I think we'll manage that.

[JENKINSON *smiles.*]

NEUBAUER: To work. Werner gets here with the prototype
tomorrow. We'll talk about the car then. The route. [*A
map*] We'll have pits at all the control points; Ravenna,
Pescara, Roma, Firenze, Bologna, Mantua. Then the home
straight back to Brescia. Now — refuelling... If you have
enough petrol to get you to Rome... etc.

6. THE INTERIOR OF A CAFÉ IN A SMALL VILLAGE NEAR
MODENA. EARLY MARCH. DAY

MOSS *and* JENKINSON *are having lunch. They are being served by
a good-looking young Italian woman.*
They look at her.
She goes.
JENKINSON *gives a hand signal.*

MOSS: Saucy? [*He look at the young woman and shakes his head*]
[JENKINSON *gives another signal.*]

MOSS: Dodgy? [*Shakes his head again*]
[*Another signal.*]

MOSS: Dangerous! [*Nods appreciatively, then gives a signal of
his own.*]

JENKINSON: Flat out in top gear!
[*They laugh.* JENKINSON *now throws signals rapidly at*
MOSS]

81

MOSS: S-bend swinging left-right, brake, dodgy right-hander, half
    throttle in third... slippery... full throttle in second,
    saucy, left-hander, full throttle in fourth!
    [*He sees he is being watched by a group of people including
    a priest. Everyone smiles.* MOSS *reflects and* JENKINSON
    greets them.]
PRIEST: The big race!
JENKINSON: That's correct.
PRIEST: Who is the corridore?
    [JENKINSON *indicates* MOSS.]
MOSS: Have a glass of wine with us.
PRIEST: [*Sitting*] Grazie. Which way did you come?
JENKINSON: From Bologna. We're on our way to Brescia.
PRIEST: Outside Modena, a bridge, an old bridge... do you
    remember it? About ten kilometres outside Modena.
    [JENKINSON *checks through a notebook.*]
MOSS: Yes, I do.
JENKINSON: Here it is. [*Reading*] Narrow, bad surface, then a
    gentle S-bend left-right, and after that first view of
    Modena.
PRIEST: No, the other side. [*Pointing to the notebook*] What does
    it say?
JENKINSON: [*Reading*] Five kilometres straight... [*Explaining*]
    A straight road for five kilometres.
PRIEST: [*He understands*] Yes, yes.
JENKINSON: [*Reading*]... four kilometres before the bridge a
    a village off the road on the right...
PRIEST: [*Nodding with a smile*] Malfi!
JENKINSON: ... you can see a church spire ... half a kilometre
    further a grove of olive trees on the left...
PRIEST: Yes, stop! You are going too fast. You will pass it. Just
    there. You can stop under those trees. The place is just a
    little bit further, just past the thirteen kilometre stone. You
    can go back to the trees and sit in the shade and think
    about it.
    [*Pause.* MOSS *and* JENKINSON *stare at him. He cannot
    believe they do not know what he is talking about.*]
PRIEST: Nuvolari. Tazio Nuvolari. That is where I found him
    crying. The Mille Miglia of 1947. Terrible! An old man!

82

His head in his hands, crying like a baby and coughing up blood... [*He pats his chest*] The disease that killed his sons. And the car! He couldn't look at it. I don't know which had the greatest shame, the man or the car. He had broken them both. The windscreen was cracked, springs broken, mudguards gone, the seat thrown out... there was a bag of oranges. For the last seventy kilometres he had driven sitting on a bag of oranges. And then outside Modena... finished! Broken! And Nuvolari cried and spat up the blood. Behind him was Ascari, Biondetti, Cortese. Leading! In that car. We put him to bed in the village. He was a sick man, shivering and coughing. And tired, inside, very tired. People say he was driving to kill himself. Just before he lay down he looked at me. "It is very difficult for a racing driver," he said, "molto difficile." Then stop, I said. He shook his head. "I must win once more." You have won enough, I said, you are Nuvolari. He looked at me and said, "That's all there is left." What? I said. All — just to win a game? "Yes." He was serious! "To win a game." We talked again the next day before they came to fetch him. I asked him if he wasn't frightened, just a little bit, to get into his car before a race. "Do you expect to die in your bed, father?" Yes, I said. "Then where do you find the courage to lie down at night?" This August he will be dead two years. I went to Mantua for his funeral. Fangio, Villoresi, Ascari... they walked with the coffin.

JENKINSON: I think he was the greatest racing driver of all time.

PRIEST: Yes, he was maestro.

JENKINSON: We'll look for the spot when we pass it again.

PRIEST: You must.

JENKINSON: And think of Nuvolari.

PRIEST: Of course. Tazio Nuvolari. [*Pause*] I think ... but I don't understand ...

7. THE INTERIOR OF ANOTHER CAFÉ. ABOUT THE SAME PERIOD AS THE LAST SCENE. DAY

MOSS *and* JENKINSON *are finishing their lunch.*

MOSS: Give me all of it at the church.

JENKINSON: Didn't I?

MOSS: No.

JENKINSON: I thought I did.

MOSS: I went through the corner, then you signalled the S-bend with half throttle in third afterwards.

[JENKINSON *is not convinced. He takes up a clipboard and notebook to check.*]

MOSS: To hell with those notes, boy. I'm telling you, I'm right.

JENKINSON: But even so, we've got time.

MOSS: No, we haven't. Look, Denis... [*He dips his finger in a glass of water and maps out on the table the section they are discussing.*] The straight out of the village, here's the church you're using as your landmark. [*He positions a salt cellar*] Here's the corner.

JENKINSON: [*His notes*] Dangerous, right-hander.

MOSS: ... then the S-bend and then the start of that section with bad surface. Right?

[JENKINSON *nods.* MOSS *takes a matchbox and drives it down the straight.*]

MOSS: Into the corner... [*The matchbox does a four-wheel drift*] I can't watch for signals there — because it's a long hard drift — I'm fighting the car and I'm on top of the S-bend before I know it.

JENKINSON: So at the church... [*He gives the hand signals for dangerous right-hander, followed by an S-bend swinging left-right, and then half-throttle in third.*]

MOSS: Right.

JENKINSON: [*His notes*] After that... yes, that hump. Remember? We came out of this lot into a straight lined with cypress trees — five kilometres — then the hump and dead straight afterwards. You changed down to fourth — do you want that?

MOSS: That's where we checked the road surface?

JENKINSON: Yes.

MOSS: [*A hand signal*] Keep it.

JENKINSON: Flat out.

MOSS: If it's dry.

JENKINSON: You don't think we're underestimating it?

MOSS: No.

JENKINSON: But if we are?

MOSS: We'll be in the air for a second or two.

JENKINSON: Hundred and seventy miles an hour. That could mean all of two hundred feet of flying. If we do take off like that and the wheels move even a fraction of an inch while we're in the air...

MOSS: [*A flash of impatience and anger*] I know! All right, keep it flat out, but signal dangerous as well. [JENKINSON *gives the two signals and starts making a few notes*] But only if it's absolutely dry. Pull me back if so much as a dog's peed on it. We've got to watch surfaces, Denis. We haven't done enough on that yet. If it's a good day and a hot sun this stretch won't be too bad, but further on it will be hell, boy. The Futa and Raticosa Passes. The tar will be soft, the other cars will have left oil and rubber all over it. We'll be dicing there. That's my nightmare — oil on the circuit.

[*Pause. While* JENKINSON *makes his notes,* MOSS *drives the matchbox along the route on the table.*]

MOSS: [*Suddenly*] Nine-thirty?

JENKINSON: What?

MOSS: We'll be on this stretch about nine-thirty.

JENKINSON: If we leave about seven. Ravenna at nine ... yes.

MOSS: What direction are we travelling along this straight?

JENKINSON: Almost south-east.

MOSS: The sun will be in your eyes. You might miss that church. Look — [*Takes an orange from a bowl of fruit and holds it above the salt cellar*] — as we swing into the straight.

JENKINSON: [*Lining himself up behind the matchbox*] Could be. Let's go back and check.

[MOSS *calls out in bad Italian for them to hurry with their bill.*]

MOSS: Il conto, per favore.

8. THE INTERIOR OF A HOTEL ROOM IN VITERBO. AFTER A PRACTICE RUN, EARLY APRIL. NIGHT

MOSS *is getting ready for bed — stripped to the waist in pyjama trousers.*

JENKINSON, *still in his clothes, is looking despondently at a clipboard with their timings for the day's run. He is obviously*

85

bewildered and tired. The relationship is strained, particularly on MOSS'S *side. He watches* JENKINSON *with growing frustration and resentment.*

MOSS: You're wasting your time! You can look at that from now until May the first, but it won't make any difference. We didn't do it!

JENKINSON: We got it down a minute on the third run.

MOSS: And the fourth? Stop trying to find excuses, Denis. [*Pause*] We didn't do it! Fact.

JENKINSON: All right! We didn't do it.

MOSS: Yes. [*Pause*] Down a minute! To what?

JENKINSON: Thirty-two.

MOSS: Thirty-two minutes! If we can't do better than that we might as well pack up and go home.

JENKINSON: Maybe with time, when we get the feel of the car and the road ....

MOSS: God, I wish you would stop that! Feel the car! Feel the road! Feel the system! What do you think we've been doing for two months? So today we went out and tried sixty-four miserable kilometres... and what happened?

JENKINSON: [*Quietly, almost at the end of his self-control*] Please don't say it again.

MOSS: If you'll stop trying to wrap it up and make it comfortable.

JENKINSON: I'm not.

MOSS: Then let it hurt.

[JENKINSON *gives a helpless gesture, picks up the clipboard and takes it to the table. The sight of the notes, maps and paraphernalia of their preparation for the race seems to steady him. He opens a map with the route of the Mille Miglia in red.*]

JENKINSON: Tomorrow?

[MOSS *doesn't answer and continues undressing in silence.* JENKINSON *looks at him, then back to the map. When he speaks again it is obvious that he is trying to bring their relationship back to an easy basis.*]

JENKINSON: Best to push on, I suppose. Viterbo — Sienna. We've got the Radicofani Pass in the middle of that lot. [*He looks again at* MOSS, *who continues to ignore him.*] I've got to check a few landmarks along there. [*His typed notes*]

Yes... those hairpins on the Sienna side.

MOSS: We'll do the same stretch again.

JENKINSON: [*Closing his eyes, hanging on*] There's one very dodgy one...

MOSS: Tomorrow.

JENKINSON: You don't think... it would be better to push on? We can't spend all our time on sixty kilometres! We've got to check and time ourselves over almost a thousand between now and May the first. Kling's been around six times already.

MOSS: We can forget about the lot if we don't get that sixty right.

JENKINSON: Let's at least push on to Florence and come back to it after a few days.

MOSS: We're going back tomorrow.

[*Pause.* MOSS *gets into bed.* JENKINSON *stares at him. When he speaks again, it is obvious that his self-control is becoming very ragged.*]

JENKINSON: Suppose we made a mistake and the limit for that stretch is thirty-two.

MOSS: It isn't.

JENKINSON: How do you know?

MOSS: I know! I know more certainly than I know who or what I am that the nine-tenths limit for that stretch is under twenty-nine minutes, and until we get it below that I don't give a damn about anything else.

JENKINSON: Including the race.

MOSS: Can't you get it through your thick skull that there's no race worth thinking about until we get it right? It's a test! And we're failing it. [*Pause*] I was faster on my own. We're in trouble.

JENKINSON: Not yet.

MOSS: Well, I'm telling you I am — and if you're not, I'd like to know what the hell you're doing next to me in that car. [JENKINSON *is on the point of a sharp retort, but stops himself in time. Instead he picks up his coat, puts it on and starts to move to the door.*]

MOSS: Where you going? We're not on holiday. We've got to be on the road at five again tomorrow morning. That means six hours sleep if you go to bed now. You need it.

JENKINSON: I'll be all right.

MOSS: No you won't ... not if you're tired. It will slow you down. As it is, you're not fast enough.

JENKINSON: [*Stung by the remark*] Where?

MOSS: Just not fast enough.

JENKINSON: Where did you have to wait for a signal?

MOSS: It's not a question of a signal. I started waiting from the moment we got into the car. You haven't learnt to think and react at a hundred and eighty miles an hour. [*Pause*] You're still going out?

JENKINSON: Yes! To see Viterbo ... at two miles an hour. I'm curious. I just want to see normal people doing the things normal people do.

[*He goes out, slamming the door in* MOSS'S *face.*]

9. THE SAME HOTEL ROOM IN VITERBO. AFTER ANOTHER PRACTICE RUN. EVENING

The door opens and MOSS *and* JENKINSON *come in, both still in their overalls.* JENKINSON *is without his glasses and looks gaunt and haggard. The front of his overall is dirty. His notes, clipboard, roller, etc., are in a mess. He puts these down fumblingly and slumps into a chair.*

MOSS: So, clean yourself up! You're filthy!

[JENKINSON *gets to his feet and feels his way to a washbasin in one corner of the room, stumbling against a chair.*]

MOSS: You said you would keep your spare glasses in the car. [*He goes to the table and looks at the mess of notes, etc.*] And next time you vomit, try to keep it off the notes. [JENKINSON *turns on the tap and washes his face.*]

JENKINSON: I couldn't help it. Those G-forces on the corner. Just don't think it was because you were driving fast, boy. You were hairy, Stirling. Hairy as a gorilla on those corners. And do you want to know something else? You did it deliberately. You were punishing me. Go on, deny it. Who do you think you are? God? What the hell. It doesn't matter. There won't be a next time. [*He gropes for a towel, dries his face, and then lies down on the floor.*] I'm leaving.

MOSS: You can't leave.

JENKINSON: That's what you think. Let's stop fooling ourselves.

There's no point. The system is not working. It could
have, but we haven't got what it takes.
[*Long pause.*]

MOSS: What do you mean?

JENKINSON: You know. [*Pushing himself up on an elbow. Another
spasm of anger*] You're a bastard, Stirling... making me
feel guilty! Because it's not my fault. I gave you those
signals as fast as you could drive. Faster! What the hell.
It's you. You don't trust me. We'll never get below thirty-
two minutes because you don't trust me. I was a fool not
to have seen it yesterday. But suddenly, that hump!... I
realised that there was twenty miles per hour more in the
car, but you were holding back. When I signalled straight
on flat out, you doubted. And when I realised that I felt
sick. I wanted to vomit. And I did, and lost my glasses. So
what? That was never a problem, because daredevil Moss
was nicely within the safety margin all the time. Nine-
tenths plus! [*Laughs bitterly*] We've been driving eight-
tenths all the time but you made it feel rough so as to hide
the truth. Tell me I'm wrong. [*Pause;* MOSS *can't. He sits
down at the end of his bed.*] I don't blame you. I could
make a mistake. The whole idea was impossible from the
start. You're a one-man system, Stirling. I'm going home.

MOSS: We've gone too far.

JENKINSON: No. We haven't gone far enough.

MOSS: We can't turn around to Neubauer now...

JENKINSON: I can. And you'll have to. Swallow your damned
pride. I'm sick of it, Stirling Moss! Or drive alone.

MOSS: I won't win the race.

JENKINSON: That's just too bad. I couldn't care less. Stick to the
G.P. circuits. This one isn't for you.

MOSS: No!

JENKINSON: [*Another bitter laugh*] What the hell. It had to be the
two of us, all the way, or nothing.
[*Pause*]

MOSS: It's not easy to trust a man like that.

JENKINSON: What do you think I'm doing there next to you
when you take those corners at a hundred and ten miles
an hour? Would you do that? Sit there and hang on while

somebody else was driving like that? You asked me last night what I was doing next to you in the car. It hurt, boy. And that's why. That's what I'm doing... trusting you!

MOSS: How?

[JENKINSON *blinks stupidly at the question, then a weary gesture. Pause.*]

JENKINSON: I don't know. It just happens. If I was sitting in a Porsche or behind you on a motorbike — something I'd know how to handle — I'd be scared anyway. But I'm not. I get into the car... I sit beside you, hold on tight... it just happens. I don't say to myself he won't make a mistake. I *hope* you don't. But you could. I'm not driving with God. [*Pause*]

MOSS: Give me another chance. [*Pause*] Tomorrow.

[JENKINSON *doesn't move for a few seconds, then up on his elbows to squint at* MOSS. *He can't see him clearly. Gets to his feet, gropes around on the table for his spare pair of spectacles, puts these on, then looks at* MOSS, *who meets his stare with equal honesty.*]

MOSS: What about it?

JENKINSON: All right. Tomorrow.

10. THE INTERIOR OF THE GARAGE IN BRESCIA, THE NEXT DAY. NIGHT

The prototype of the SLR 300 is up on jacks. It has been badly smashed in an accident. HUGO *and a mechanic are under it.* MOSS, *a small cut on his forehead, and* JENKINSON *are looking at the car, still in their overalls and obviously very tired. After a few seconds* NEUBAUER *comes hurriedly into the garage through a side door.*

NEUBAUER: Are you hurt?

[JENKINSON *shakes his head.*]

NEUBAUER: They just said there'd been an accident.

JENKINSON: An army lorry. No warning. Just swung across the road. We didn't stand a chance. [*Wry smile*] The soldiers jumped out and came dashing around, swearing at us. But when they saw the SLR — happy smiles and Mille Miglia! [*The car*] Bit of a mess, I'm afraid.

NEUBAUER: Cars we can always build. Drivers we are forced to

90

value. [*Goes to* MOSS]

MOSS: She's oversteering more than I thought. We can't afford to slide around that much.

NEUBAUER: Do you need a doctor?

MOSS: [*Shakes his head*] And the tyre pressure. I didn't like it. It's got to be the same all round. I didn't have enough play.

JENKINSON: The lorry was carrying dynamite.

[HUGO *slides out from under the car. He joins the three men and, with a long face, shakes his head. He and* NEUBAUER *exchange a few words in German. It is obvious that the car has to be written off.* MOSS *and* JENKINSON *sit down, side by side, on a bench.*]

NEUBAUER: I must phone Stuttgart. We will build a new one.

MOSS: We can't stop now.

NEUBAUER: Take the SL —

MOSS: Yes. Tomorrow.

NEUBAUER: Rest for a few days.

MOSS: No.

[NEUBAUER *hesitates, then finishes his instructions to the mechanic.*]

NEUBAUER: [*To* MOSS *and* JENKINSON] You'll feel better after a few days rest.

MOSS: Better? We've never felt better, Alfred. If that damned lorry hadn't got in the way we would have done the Viterbo stretch in under twenty-nine minutes!

[NEUBAUER *and* HUGO *leave. The mechanic follows.* JENKINSON *and* MOSS *are alone.*]

JENKINSON: [*Starting to unzip his overalls*] There's a lot of time in a few seconds like that. I remember thinking quite clearly... it was the same when we hit those sheep... It'll be tight, I couldn't do it, but if anyone can, he can. I wasn't frightened, just interested.

MOSS: Journalist!

JENKINSON: But it's the same with you. You don't get frightened.

MOSS: Remember my shunt at Spa? The practice was warming up. Almost everyone was out. It was a fine day. I was clocking up my third lap when it happened. The Burenville Corner — just before the Masta straight. That big hump in the middle. I was doing about a hundred and forty when I hit the hump and the wheel came off. For a few seconds I didn't know what had happened. All I knew was that suddenly the car was oversteering tremendously. Much more even than you get on oil... The most violent oversteer I had ever felt. I hadn't seen the wheel. All I could do was apply full-lock and stand on the brakes. I started to spin and then I saw the wheel. I realised I was going to hit the bank backwards, at a good ninety miles an hour. I braced myself and the last thing I remember was my head jerking back as the car clouted the edge. When I came round I was out of the car... on my hands and knees. I couldn't have been unconscious long because before it all happened I'd passed Bruce Maclaren. I knew he would stop as soon as he saw the accident. He wasn't there yet. What was really worring me was that I couldn't breathe. Hell, I felt lonely, boy. I couldn't think why Bruce was taking so long. But then he came... just suddenly there. I asked him to give me artificial respiration but he was scared to, in case I had broken ribs. Then all the other drivers started to arrive. That corner must have looked like a car park. And hot. Hot as hell. Somebody found a blanket and held it over me to keep off the sun. They cut the elastic at my wrists, took off my watch. All the time this was going on I could hear their voices, but I couldn't see them. My eyes were open but everything was dark. I was really frightened that I had done something to my eyes... that I had gone blind or something. I knew I had messed up my legs. Then the ambulance arrived and they gave me an injection. Just before I passed out I remembered seeing the wheel. You don't know what that meant. It hadn't been my fault! I wouldn't have raced again if it had been. I wouldn't have had enough courage. [*He climbs into the car.*]

I'm afraid of death. But I don't think about it. When I get into the car I say to myself... let's try to drive the perfect lap. Just once! All the way around and not one mistake... not one mile an hour too slow or ten revs down! Sometimes it almost happens. You go through a corner absolutely flat out, right on the ragged edge, but absolutely in control of your own line to an inch... the car just hanging there, the tyres as good as geared to the road. And yet you know that if you push it up just one more mile an hour, put just another five pounds of side thrust on it, you'll lose the car as surely as if someone had smeared six inches of grease on the road. When you're doing that you say to yourself: All right, you bastards! Top that one! And when it's like that, it's good, boy. Pleasure... fulfilment... a sense of achievement.[*Pause*] But there's more to it than that. Racing cars aren't happiness machines.

[*Pan down to the crashed wing of the SLR 300.*]

11. THE SAME.

The car as before, but this time a mechanic is busy painting the number 722 in large red numerals across the bonnet.

NEUBAUER: Let us not fool ourselves, gentlemen. The draw has not made it easier for us. The Ferraris have four of the last six places. On top of that he is not going to announce until the last moment which driver will be in which car. It is a good trick. We will not let it upset us, or our plans. If necessary we will re-examine the situation when they announce their placings. So, our numbers... Fangio 658, Kling 701, Hermann 704 and Moss 722. The Ferrari numbers... 705, 720, 723, 727... and the last to leave, 728. There are over five hundred cars in the race this year. They start leaving at nine tomorrow night.

12. INTERIOR. HOTEL SUITE, BRESCIA. DAY. EARLY MARCH —
SECOND DISCUSSION

MOSS *and* JENKINSON *amid a welter of maps, papers, etc.*

MOSS: Okay, fine. Let's call them saucy, dodgy and dangerous. It gives them character.

[JENKINSON *notes down the headings.*]

JENKINSON: [*Notes*] So, for example...

MOSS: That stretch we looked at today. Take it from Viterbo.

JENKINSON: [*Reading*] Left-hander...

MOSS: That's easy.

JENKINSON: ... three kilometres straight, left-hander again...

MOSS: Saucy.

JENKINSON: Then the sharp right-hander.

MOSS: Dodgy.

[JENKINSON *twists his head to read something from his notes.*]

JENKINSON: Yes. You had to change down. And dangerous?

MOSS: Radicofani Pass. On this side, coming down. It will be hell over that lot if it rains.

JENKINSON: And that one after Acquapendente. Remember it? [*Struggling again to read his notes*] "Right-hander..." It's murder trying to write at a hundred and forty miles an hour... "Right-hander, bad surface." That's the one.

MOSS: Dangerous.

JENKINSON: What about a fourth category... between dodgy and dangerous. Very dodgy.

MOSS: Such as?

JENKINSON: The Rome side of the Radicofani.

MOSS: [*Shakes his head*] Dodgy or dangerous. There's nothing in between. When I've got the fat part of a whole second to start my drift — they're just dodgy.

JENKINSON: Okay. [*He gets up from his chair with a groan, his hand to his back*] At this rate I'll be wearing a corset before the end. You've at least got the steering wheel to hang on to.

MOSS: Ask Alfred to put in one for you. [*Laughing*] Can you see Costellotti's face when we pass him? Both of us driving!

JENKINSON: [*Sheet of paper*] Here's the list. The road: Corners, saucy, dodgy and dangerous, S-bends. Bad surfaces: bumpy, slippery, level crossing, bridge, sudden dip. Directions: Left, right, straight on. The car: brake, full throttle, half throttle, first gear, second, third, fourth and fifth.

MOSS: Twenty.

JENKINSON: Anything missing?

MOSS: We'll find out soon enough.

13. THE SAME. THE FOLLOWING DAY

JENKINSON: This is what I thought.

[MOSS *looks up.*]

MOSS: Hold on — wait a minute. Start again.

[JENKINSON *goes through his list with a signal for each item.*]

JENKINSON: Corners... saucy... dodgy... dangerous... S-bend, left-right... S-bend, right-left. [MOSS *nods*] The road: bumpy... slippery... level crossing... bridge... sudden dip. [MOSS *nods*] Directions: left... right... straight on.

MOSS: Straight on. [*Amends signal*]

[JENKINSON *makes a note, and looks up.*]

JENKINSON: Left... right... straight on... Car: brake... half throttle... full throttle... first... second... third... fourth... fifth. Okay?

MOSS: Fine. What were those corners? [JENKINSON *illustrating*] Saucy... dodgy... dangerous. Yes, fine. Look, let's try it out. [JENKINSON *reacts*] That corner — the dangerous one... outside Acquapendente.

JENKINSON: What do you think it's going to be?

MOSS: I want to feel it again, but let's say half throttle in second.

JENKINSON: Right. We're coming to it.

MOSS: No — wait a minute — here.

[*He gets up. They move seats.*
JENKINSON *gives the signal.* MOSS *interpreting.*]

MOSS: Dangerous right-hander. [*Another signal from* JENKINSON] Half throttle. [*Another signal*] In second. Great. Don't make any mistakes, boy.

JENKINSON: Not if I can help it. I'll be sitting next to you, remember. Here they are again. [*Goes through signals*]

MOSS: S-bend... swinging left... full throttle... slippery... surface... bridge... sudden dip...

14. THE SAME. A MONTH BEFORE THE RACE. NIGHT
JENKINSON *is at the table. With pen and ink he is carefully transcribing the last of their route notes on to a length of paper about six inches wide and nineteen feet long. The paper is blank for about a foot at either end.*
While JENKINSON *is busy,* MOSS *toys with the specially made roller — an adaptation of the roller map idea. The paper will wind off the bottom spool on to the top one, the notes sliding past under a perspex window.*
JENKINSON: Thirty kilometres straight to Brescia.

MOSS: Rome's going to be the worst. The outskirts. They usually keep them under control over the last mile into the control point. But until then it's going to be sheer hell.

JENKINSON: [*Looking up briefly*] Hundred and fifty miles an hour into Rome.

MOSS: With a human wall on both sides. If only they'd keep back! But they go mad. They don't seem to have any idea of the danger involved. One day [*Shakes his head*] — no! Just keep that horn and lights going. I'll swing the car a bit from side to side. I did it last time. It seemed to help. That's all we can do... and then hope there isn't some idiot dancing about on the round around the next corner. Five million people, Denis — it only takes one fool — two of us, five million of them.

[*He goes into the bedroom, where he opens the roller, takes out the bottom spool and,* JENKINSON *joining him, they carefully roll on the paper.* MOSS *attaches the free end to the top spool, closes the case and starts to wind.* JENKINSON'S *notes slide past under the window.*]

MOSS: Perfect.

JENKINSON: Let me try.

MOSS: We'd better seal it around the edges here with tape or something, just in case it rains.

JENKINSON: Yes.

MOSS: Okay?

JENKINSON: Okay.

MOSS: Let's go.

[MOSS *goes through to the lounge and he takes two chairs and puts them side by side.* JENKINSON *follows.*
JENKINSON *sits on one chair and puts the roller on his knee. He looks up.* MOSS *sits alongside.*]

JENKINSON: Piazza Vittorio. We're on the ramp. Goggles on. I show you the note reminding you to be easy on the brakes through the first corners.

MOSS: Fine.

JENKINSON: Starter raises his flag. Thirty seconds.

MOSS: I've started the engine.

JENKINSON: The flag is down.

MOSS: Here we go. Down the Via Trieste, right at the bottom into the square, across it . . .

JENKINSON: We know this bit backwards. Let's pick it up out of town . . . [*Winding the roller*] The end of that seven kilometre stretch, with the canal on the side. Ready?

[JENKINSON *nods.* MOSS *gives his first signal.*]

MOSS: [*Easily*] S-bend left-right, full throttle in fourth, flat out afterwards.

JENKINSON: Into a three-kilometre straight . . . one . . . two . . . three. Cemetery coming up on the right. [*Another signal*]

MOSS: Dodgy right-hander, full throttle in third . . . straight into fifth flat out.

JENKINSON: Olive trees! [*Signal; pause*]

MOSS: Dumpy surface . . . change down to third . . . [*Signal*] Back to fifth . . . full throttle . . .

JENKINSON: Long straight! One . . . two . . . three . . . four . . . five . . .

15. ABOUT TEN MINUTES LATER

They are still in their chairs. A heightened sensation of speed.
JENKINSON *is turning the roller and signalling faster.* MOSS'S
voice is louder and more urgent as he interprets the signals.

MOSS: Down to third! Saucy right hander . . . [*Signals*] Flat out.

JENKINSON: Six kilometres straight ending at the eighteen kilometre stone. Watch for it! . . . fourteen . . . sixteen . . . seventeen . . . [*Signal*]

MOSS: Level crossing!

JENKINSON: [*Looking to left and right*] Okay . . . clear! [*Signal*]

MOSS: Flat out! We're through.

JENKINSON: San Paolo coming up. We can see it. [*Signal*]

MOSS: Brake! Going into the village on a right-hand curve at half-throttle . . .

16. THE SAME

Still driving. Still more heightened sensation of speed.

JENKINSON: . . . nineteen . . . twenty . . . I can see the house coming! So can you! . . . twenty-one . . . twenty-two . . . [*Signal*]

MOSS: [*Now shouting*] Dangerous right-hander, half throttle in second . . . straight into the S-bend, swinging left-right . . .

Change up! Third! Fourth!

JENKINSON: One kilometre straight... you can see the road.
Dodgy right-hander coming up... S-bend... you can see
all that... but you can't see this! [*Signal*]

MOSS: Dodgy right-hander?

JENKINSON: We're in the straight! Railway line on our left.
[*Signal*]

MOSS: Level crossing in fourth!

JENKINSON: Clear!

MOSS: We're through.

JENKINSON: Into Ravenna...

MOSS: Control point. We're coming to it. Brakes... slowing
down...

JENKINSON: Route card ready... holding out my hand to show
which side we want him... card's over the side. [*He does
all this*]... he's running beside us... bang... stamp is
on... [*Signal*]

MOSS: Full throttle!

17. THE SAME

*They are now rehearsing signals, etc., at the top speed of the
SLR 300.*

JENKINSON: ... seven... eight... nine... ten... eleven...
twelve.

MOSS: One hundred and eighty miles an hour.

JENKINSON: ... thirteen... fourteen... fifteen... sixteen.
Honk! Honk!

MOSS: I'm swinging! They're jumping back.

JENKINSON: Honk! Honk! Last mile into the control point —
crowd's behind barriers now. Let them know we're
coming! Honk! Honk! Control point coming up.

MOSS: Braking!

JENKINSON: [*Going through the earlier drill with the route card*]
Bang! It's on. There's the flag. Pit stop!

MOSS: We're in!
[*Zoom out; they both jump out of their chairs. They stand,
panting and staring at each other.*]

MOSS: [*Suddenly*] It's started to rain.

JENKINSON: All the way!

98

MOSS: Yes.

JENKINSON: Right.

MOSS: It's ready. [*They jump in*] Here we go! Into that hairpin after the control point...

JENKINSON: Honk! Honk!...

18. THE SAME

JENKINSON: Acquapendente!

MOSS: Into the square... four wheel drift coming up... full throttle... wheel and brakes... We're sliding... sliding... wheel and brakes... starting to hold... we're through.

JENKINSON: Waiting for the church... there it is... here we go! [*Signal*]

MOSS: [*Shouting*] Dangerous right-hander half throttle in third! [*Signal*] Full throttle in fourth! [*Signal*] Slippery surface... half throttle in third. [*Signal*] S-bend swinging left-right. [*Signal*] Brake... down to second. [*Signal*] Dangerous left-hander... slippery??!

[JENKINSON *has suddenly stopped signalling and is staring at the roller.*]

MOSS: Mistake?

JENKINSON: [*Nodding*] That last corner... was a right-hander. [*Pause*] I'm sure I —

MOSS: Too late! Doesn't matter who did it, boy. We're dead!

19. THE SAME

Another rehearsal in chairs with the roller.

MOSS: [*Shouting*] Road is slippery... melted tar... oil patches... we're dicing... [JENKINSON *signals*] Bridge coming up... down to fourth, half throttle... [*Signal*] Dodgy left-hander... flat out in top afterwards.

JENKINSON: Do you know what that was?

MOSS: Again?!! [*Face and body rigid with anticipation, as he misunderstands the question*]

JENKINSON: [*Quickly*] No! [*He pauses*] That was my last signal.

MOSS: What?

JENKINSON: [*Putting away the roller*] We are thirty kilometres from Brescia. It's a straight all the way.

[*They stare at each other for a few seconds, then start to*

99

laugh. Their relief is enormous.]

MOSS: If she blows up now we'll carry her the rest of the way! Well done!

[*At the height of their excitement,* MOSS *slaps* JENKINSON *on the back. The latter's glasses fall off. There is silence as he feels around and finds them on the floor.*]

JENKINSON: [*Trying to change the subject*] That wasn't so bad.

MOSS: Keep them in the car. [JENKINSON *stares at him*] Your spare glasses.

JENKINSON: What do you take me for?

MOSS: I'm just saying.

JENKINSON: No you're not! Look, Stirling, if you want a passenger without glasses why don't you say so!

MOSS: Take it easy, boy.

JENKINSON: [*Pulling himself together*] Sorry. [*The roller*] That felt like a thousand miles.

[*They get out of their chairs stiffly. It is now obvious just how exhausting the rehearsal has been.*]

JENKINSON: Suppose the car does break down somewhere... something we can't fix... how far are we prepared to push it to a control point?

MOSS: [*Doing a few exercises to loosen up*] I pushed my Maserati half a mile at Monza. If I'd had to I would have pushed it a mile. I'll double that this time.

JENKINSON: I'll do the same. Four miles.

MOSS: Let's make it five.

JENKINSON: Okay.

MOSS: To a control point or the finish. Whatever else happens, let's try to finish.

JENKINSON: [*Idly turning the roller*] But it did feel all right, didn't it?

MOSS: Sitting still, yes. Now let's get into the car.

JENKINSON: Tomorrow.

MOSS: Yeah. Tomorrow. Of course. [*Goes to the wardrobe*]

JENKINSON: Where do we start?

MOSS: Rome-Florence. If the car's going to break up anywhere it will be somewhere along there. Thirty gallons of petrol behind us, bad surfaces...

JENKINSON: And an average of ninety plus.

MOSS: [*Pointing to the map*] That Viterbo stretch. What's our practice target?

JENKINSON: Do you want to start timing?

MOSS: Might as well. What time have we set ourselves for that stretch?

JENKINSON: [*A notebook*] Twenty-two minutes.
[JENKINSON *is suddenly thoughtful.*]

MOSS: What's on your mind?

JENKINSON: Nothing.

MOSS: [*A spark of irritation*] Come on, boy!
[JENKINSON *takes off his glasses, making a big thing of cleaning them.*]

JENKINSON: Well, I thought we were going to cruise the whole circuit first — a last check... landmarks, some of those corners we think might need regrading...

MOSS: Of course. We'll do all that. But what's wrong with doing a bit of driving at the same time.

JENKINSON: Okay, fine. [*Going to the bedroom*] I just thought that if before we got down to business we could have checked everything slowly, just once... [MOSS *shrugs*] Well, it would have given us confidence in the system.

MOSS: But I've got it. Look, Denis, the system is fine, but for hell's sake there is also a limit to it... to any system for that matter. You're on the ball, my reflexes are sharp, the road is dry and the car is giving us seven and a half thousand revs so we take that corner flat out because everything is just perfect, and as we come out of the corner we find a one-cylinder Isotta on its side slap in the middle of the road! I know it's a pretty system. But it's supposed to be a tool, not a toy. I've done enough playing. Now I want to work and tomorrow that means driving. [*Goes to the bathroom*]

JENKINSON: I just don't know that I'm ready yet.

MOSS: Yes you are! We're not going to take on the whole route! I just want to get the feel of about sixty kilometres.

JENKINSON: Driving nine-tenths.
[MOSS *comes out of the bathroom, goes to the cupboard.*]

MOSS: Yes. Tell you what, we'll go over it once slowly, and then have a crack at our target.

JENKINSON: All right.

> [MOSS *gets out a suitcase and starts packing a few things.* JENKINSON *sits down with the roller and turns it to the section that they will do the next day.*]

20. INTERIOR OF A COMFORTABLE HOTEL SUITE IN BRESCIA. THE NIGHT BEFORE THE RACE, APRIL 30TH, 8.00 P.M.

There is a lounge, a bedroom with two beds, and leading off that a bathroom. On a table in the lounge is JENKINSON'S *typewriter, notebooks, papers, etc., and the special roller they will use in the next day's race. Next to this, in an orderly pile, are their personal requisites for the race — a dozen packets of sucking sweets, two bottles of orange juice, bananas, a spare pair of spectacles for* JENKINSON, *spare gloves for* MOSS, *etc.*

JENKINSON, *alone, is in an easy chair trying to read a paper. After a few moments he gets up, goes to the radio, looks at his watch, realises it's not time for the start. Then, aimlessly, to the bedroom. Two crash helmets on a bed. He goes out on to the balcony.*

After a moment, a decisive move to the lounge. He goes to the phone and asks the exchange for a number.

JENKINSON: Quattrocento, per favore... Hugo? Yes... is he there? No, nothing... What? They have? Wait! [*Puts down the phone and fetches pencil and paper*] Okay... [*Waiting*] Yes... Yes... Yes... [*A little laugh as he writes down the last name and number*] Obviously. Okay, fine. I suppose he'll be here soon.

> [*He hangs up. Looks thoughtfully at the names and numbers.* MOSS *comes in.*]

MOSS: Have you heard?

JENKINSON: The Ferrari placings?

MOSS: They've put Costellotti behind us, Maglioli behind Hermann. Then Marzotto and last of all Taruffi.

JENKINSON: Hugo told me. I phoned the garage.

MOSS: We had a session with Alfred, team briefing. He's sticking to his plan.

JENKINSON: So we go flat out and try and burn up the Ferraris.

MOSS: Leaving it clear for Fangio and Kling to drive their own races. Well, we'll see about that. [JENKINSON *watches him and smiles*] So that's that.

JENKINSON: Looks like it.

MOSS: Otherwise everything's in order.

JENKINSON: Good.

MOSS: Did you take your walk?

JENKINSON: Yes. I've been back about an hour. There's some coffee and sandwiches coming up. Ham.

MOSS: How's your stomach?

JENKINSON: Fine. It will be okay. And you? Tired?

MOSS: I think so. I'll turn in after a shower. Get a good night.

JENKINSON: You're not going to wait for the start? An hour to go?

MOSS: If I'm still awake ... but I don't want to think. I don't want to think.

JENKINSON: Of course.

[*Pause. Then* MOSS *goes into the bedroom.*]

MOSS: Anything in the paper?

JENKINSON: *Dello Sport* says Costellotti's going to win tomorrow, from Taruffi and Fangio. *Gazzetta Sportiva* says "Epico Duello tra Fangio e Taruffi".

[*A laugh from* MOSS *in the bathroom.*]

MOSS: What's wrong with me? [*In bedroom, taking off shoes*]

JENKINSON: Too rough on the car. You won't last the distance.

[MOSS *comes back into the room.*]

MOSS: Am I? [*At door, undoing shirt*]

JENKINSON: No. Certainly not now. Hard maybe ... as hard on yourself, and me, as you are on the car. Even that's the wrong word. You just ask for a lot. You're plain greedy.

MOSS: [*Back in bedroom*] That link mechanism works perfectly. We won't have any trouble with the gears.

JENKINSON: You went out?

MOSS: Just a few kilometres.

JENKINSON: This evening?

MOSS: We've only checked it once. I just wanted to make sure. [*A little defensively*] I sometimes do it, on a G.P. circuit. Just go out and cruise it once after the practice laps. I don't know. Feel it in slow motion, I suppose. But that's a formula car. That was the difference this afternoon. It didn't feel the same. I mean, the SLR has got two seats. I missed you, boy.

[*He leaves the room.* JENKINSON *puts down the paper.* MOSS
turns on the shower. JENKINSON *looks towards the
bathroom.*

MOSS *vigorous under the shower.*

JENKINSON *takes out a notebook, studies notes about the
car.* JENKINSON *looks up.*]

MOSS: [*To the bed*] ... the only time it interests me is when I'm in it
and it's travelling fast. As a device it bores me. People on
the outside don't understand. But it's true. A racing driver
doesn't really care which way the gear works. Or even
what gear he's in. You don't wait for valve bounce to
know it's time to change. You just know the thing has
come to a point where it can't put out any more power in
the gear it's in, so you go looking for another one, and
quickly!

[*Knock on the door.*]

JENKINSON: Ham?

WAITER: [*Entering*] Si.

JENKINSON: The same tomorrow.

WAITER: At half-past five. [*The tray is down. He hesitates at the
door before leaving*] What is your starting time?

JENKINSON: Seven twenty-two.

WAITER: Castellotti?

JENKINSON: Seven twenty-three.

WAITER: Right behind you! The favourite.

JENKINSON: Yes.

WAITER: I have a ticket in the lottery.

JENKINSON: You'd like to draw him.

WAITER: Castellotti! Si! ... If he wins, a hundred million lire!

JENKINSON: Good luck.

[*The waiter leaves.* JENKINSON *pours himself a cup of tea.*]

21. THE SAME.

JENKINSON *with his tea and sandwiches.*

JENKINSON: Fangio 658, Kling 701, Collins, 702, Maglioli 705,
Scotti 718, Carini ... [*Pause. He looks up and thinks, then
checks his list*] Carini 714, Pinzero 720 ...

[MOSS *comes into the room, drying himself.*]

JENKINSON: Taruffi must be wondering if this is going to be his year.

MOSS: [*Going to balcony*] Last off the mark.

JENKINSON: And his twelfth attempt. He's a good driver and he's intelligent. People don't appreciate that. It's not spectacular enough, I suppose. But he always knows his circuit, his machine, and a master tactician... and strong! The size of those forearms! [MOSS *comes back into the room.*]

MOSS: Costellotti one minute behind us.

JENKINSON: Yes. That's going to be interesting.

MOSS: And Marzotto.

JENKINSON: I think we've got to reckon on Costellotti passing us somewhere. He's got a lot of power under the bonnet of that Ferrari... and you know what he drives like.

MOSS: Anything can happen, boy. But I suppose you're right. Where?

JENKINSON: Somewhere between Rimini and Pescara. I think we'll be able to dice it out with him until then, but once we get on to those long stretches it's going to be a question of sheer horsepower. After Pescara it will be a different story, in the mountains around Aquila and Rieti... he'll have to drive there.

MOSS: Well, we'll have to try to hang on to him until then.

JENKINSON: Coffee?

MOSS: Thanks. We checked the weather forecast again just before I left. It looks good.

JENKINSON: It will be perfect. It's impossible to imagine otherwise.

[*Pause.* MOSS *moves suddenly.*]

MOSS: Right. Let's get that on record. Where's m'book? [*He settles down with his diary and pen.*] April thirtieth... [*Starts to write*] D. predicts perfect weather. [*Looking up*] A fast race?

JENKINSON: A fast race.

MOSS: [*Writing*] And a fast race.

JENKINSON: Could you imagine rain tomorrow?

MOSS: Forecasts have been wrong before. Might even want it before the day's over. [*Pause*] It will be hot in that car once the sun's really up. Hundred and thirty plus. [*He goes on writing.*]

JENKINSON: Just a feeling during my walk, that things like bad weather, getting up late... being allowed to make mistakes... [MOSS *looks at him and smiles*] They'll all start again after tomorrow. Tomorrow has to, and will be, perfect... the weather, the car, you know... and maybe me. It's a rarefied atmosphere.

MOSS: You're acclimatised.

JENKINSON: More than I was. I haven't really realised until now all that was involved in being inside that cockpit, inside the experience rather than standing on the side and watching it. I thought I did. My stint with Eric Oliver in the side-car championships. All the times I've seen you go up to the grid, get in and then wait for the flag to drop, and watched you dice it out for a couple of hours... I thought I knew what was happening, but I didn't really.

MOSS: If you don't who does?

JENKINSON: You. The driver. That's the difference. I'm a passenger. [MOSS *looks up at him*] That's what the regulations call me. And you don't have to have one. Taruffi drives alone.

MOSS: So?

JENKINSON: If something happened to me, you'd still race tomorrow. Wouldn't you?

MOSS: What does that prove? [JENKINSON *doesn't reply*] Sure, I could drive a thousand miles without you, but I wouldn't win. There were lots of people who wanted to go along on this ride, Denis. I didn't put all the names in a hat and pull yours out. I *chose* you. There was no one else. [*Goes back to his diary*]

JENKINSON: A thousand miles to get nowhere.

MOSS: That's right. And I want to be there first.

22. THE SAME

JENKINSON *eats his sandwich, watching* MOSS *who is still writing.*

JENKINSON: I took my walk along the river. [*Pause*] I only got as far as the cathedral. I don't know... there was nothing outside there for me. It was like that night in Viterbo — remember... normal people doing normal things. I never

106

told you about it. But then, and this time again... it felt as if I was on the outside looking in... or the inside looking out, in the cockpit, passing it all so fast I could never be a part... What they don't understand is the way it works. What frightens and what doesn't frighten a racing driver.

MOSS: I've been frightened plenty of times.

JENKINSON: But not of a crash?

MOSS: [*Drinking coffee*] No. You live with that. No, I suppose it was afterwards... when I've woken up in a hospital bed, and realised how close it was to being the end of everything. I've experienced more fright lying flat on my back, remembering...

JENKINSON: ... than in the cockpit?

MOSS: There isn't time for it then. [*He sits*]

JENKINSON: It's more than that, surely. It's anticipation — the difference between the known and the unknown.

MOSS: I'm not with you.

JENKINSON: When we hit that lorry outside Viterbo. You saw it coming. And not just in terms of that couple of seconds. We'd been expecting some fool to do something like that sooner or later. It was a probability.

MOSS: See what you mean.

JENKINSON: In all the spins and crashes I've been in, I don't think I've ever frozen up. They've all been anticipated. Maybe by just a fraction of a second. But I saw them coming. The sort of thing that really does frighten me is when something happens out of the blue. [*A little laugh as he remembers*] One night I was on my motorbike. I didn't realise I was riding next to railway lines. Suddenly this train came out of the tunnel with a hell of a roar. I swerved so violently I nearly fell off the bike. No danger, understand. Just fright. The unanticipated... the unknown. If the motor had burst underneath me with a noise just as loud, I would have coped. [MOSS *smiles*] Like that night I had the nightmare and fell out of bed, and you leapt up shouting, "What's happened? What's happened?" That was the only time I've ever seen you look frightened.

107

[MOSS *smiles again, and goes back to his diary.*]

23. THE SAME

MOSS *looks up from his diary to find* JENKINSON *staring at him.*

MOSS: Something on your mind?

JENKINSON: What happened to you today?

MOSS: Nothing. Why?

JENKINSON: [*The diary*] And all that?

MOSS: [*Looking over what he has just written*] Car down to
   Piazzo Vittorio for the inspection... chat with Mike...
   he'll be driving for Maserati at Le Mans... our starting
   number... weather forecast... our chances... [*Looking up
   at* JENKINSON] I've put them at fair. [*The diary*] That's all.
   The things I'll forget. Remind me that April 30th was also
   a day in my life. I'd never remember otherwise.

JENKINSON: You'll be up all tomorrow night writing.

MOSS: No. I won't need it then. I never forget a race.

JENKINSON: How many races this year?

MOSS: Twenty... twenty-five.

JENKINSON: Twenty-five days a year you don't forget.

MOSS: That's right. Do you do better?

JENKINSON: No. [MOSS *goes back to the balcony*] You think
   Fangio will listen. To the start?

MOSS: Don't know. He's awake. He won't sleep tonight. I'll take
   on any odds he didn't sleep last night either. It's the same
   every time. On top of it he hates this race. Says one day
   he'll have enough courage to turn around and say, "No
   thank you, it's too dangerous." Kling and Hermann have
   a beer, I suppose. The Ferrari boy's getting a last word
   from 'Il Commendatore'. Peter's asleep. [*A small laugh*]...
   and Taruffi's polishing his engine. He's going to win it one
   day.

JENKINSON: Waiting.

MOSS: What?

JENKINSON: You, Fangio, Rauffi... all the others.

MOSS: What else is there to do? We race tomorrow.

JENKINSON: That's what I mean. The cars are ready... you could
   go out there now and do it... but there's a starting time,
   rules...

MOSS: There's no game without rules. The trouble is most people who play games don't understand the rules. I've got a theory about them... the rules. Cheating is out, under any circumstances, but on the other hand I think it's perfectly fair to play so close to them that you couldn't get a razor blade into the crack. But to do that you've got to know them. Ever tell you about the time with Masten Gregory in Havana?

JENKINSON: No.

MOSS: There was a lot of oil on the circuit, so I let Masten pass into first place. [JENKINSON *laughs*] Sounds like a first-class bastard, I know.

JENKINSON: Some people would think so.

MOSS: Anyway, I was going to let him find the oil. I stayed on his tail. Then someone else had a bad accident and a marshal put out the red flag. Masten stood on everything and slowed down. I also started to slow down but then I remembered that the regulations stipulated that the red flag was only valid if shown by the clerk of the course, and at the finish line. So I stuck it into second, jumped on the throttle and ran past Masten to win. He was sore as hell. Reckoned I had cheated him out of winning. I told him... if you don't know the regs, Masten, you must expect to be beaten by somebody who does. But I said I'd split first prize money with him if he'd split second prize with me. Sixty seconds dead...

JENKINSON: Would you like...

MOSS: What?

JENKINSON: Nothing. I just wondered if you'd like to run over a couple of the difficult bits. Radicofani...

MOSS: It's too late for that, boy.

JENKINSON: Yes, of course... Oh, I got you the sweets you like.

MOSS: Lemon?

JENKINSON: Well, I got assorted, but there'll be lemon among them.

MOSS: Fine, fine...

24. THE SAME

JENKINSON *is at the table, staring at the roller.* MOSS, *in a chair, is playing with a stopwatch. Someone is knocking at the door.*

JENKINSON: [*A fraction too loudly and eagerly*] Come in!

[*The waiter comes in.* MOSS *starts the watch.*]

WAITER: Are you finished?

JENKINSON: Yes.

[*The waiter goes to the table to clear away the tray.* MOSS *and* JENKINSON *watch him.* MOSS *has the stopwatch going. The waiter seems to take an interminable time. He looks up once or twice, self-conscious of the scrutiny, and smiles. Finally, he is at the door on his way out.*]

WAITER: Good luck.

[MOSS *stops the watch as the door shuts.*]

MOSS: Forty seconds.

[JENKINSON *nods, equally serious in his appreciation of this piece of information.*]

MOSS: Three point two kilometres at our fastest!

25. THE SAME

MOSS *comparing his wristwatch with the stopwatch.*

26. THE SAME

JENKINSON *is standing quite still, staring at the roller. He then moves abruptly, almost desperately, as he tries to escape from the memory of the next few minutes of their rehearsal. He moves to a small portable radio.* MOSS *still with the stopwatch.*

MOSS: Is it time?

[JENKINSON *on the point of turning on the radio. He stops and looks at his watch.*]

JENKINSON: No. Not quite.

[JENKINSON *goes to the bathroom.*]

MOSS: Round and round. This lump of mud and rock, or whatever it is we're living on, is turning at a good thousand miles an hour or so. That's what governs us. If you don't keep moving... you're dead.

27. INTERIOR. BATHROOM

JENKINSON *in the bathroom, brushing his teeth vigorously. He stops and stares at himself in the mirror above the wash-*

basin. MOSS *is talking in the other room.*

MOSS: Neubauer doesn't agree at all. But as far as I am concerned
a pit is all the better for a bit of crumpet around.
Somebody to wave to, take your mind off things... even if
it's just the moment when you come in half a lap ahead
with the transmission in bits. [*Sits on bed*]
[JENKINSON *moves to the bathroom door where he stands
and watches* MOSS *unobserved. The latter is laying out his
racing clothes, overalls, helmet, goggles, soft suede shoes,
etc.*]

MOSS: I used to discipline myself too severely. Wouldn't even look
at a woman for days before a race. But hell, I mean, if it's
got to be like that, why live at all? I used to think that if I
had a bit the night before a race, I would be physically
just that little bit weaker when I drove... reflexes a
fraction of a second slower. That's all it needs. Then one
night at Brands Hatch there was a girl. Hm. I had seven
races the next day — only short ones, mind you — but I
won the lot!
[*He is now dusting talcum powder into his underpants he will
wear the next day.* JENKINSON, *still unobserved, goes back
into the bathroom.*]

28. THE SAME

JENKINSON *sits down on the edge of the bath.* MOSS *is still
talking in the other room.*

MOSS: I haven't altogether changed my mind. Before a really big
race — like tomorrow, or Le Mans, Sevring — no.

29. INTERIOR. BEDROOM

MOSS: There's no sex in driving as far as I'm concerned.
Stimulation, yes. Tremendous. But non-physical. And
tranquillity. Does that seem strange? Sounds a bit
paradoxical, I know, speed and peace. But it's true, like a
gramophone record, the nearer you get to the centre, the
slower the thing is moving. Maybe right at the centre,
nothing is moving at all. The nearest I'll ever get to real
peace is when I'm driving very fast.

30. INTERIOR. BATHROOM

JENKINSON *remembers the row in Viterbo. Their voices on the soundtrack. Visuals from Scenes 8 and 9.*

31. THE SAME

JENKINSON *in the bathroom as we last saw him, sitting at the end of the bath.* MOSS *is in the doorway.*

MOSS: It's time. Denis!

[JENKINSON *looks at his watch.*]

JENKINSON: So it is.

[*Goes into the lounge to fetch the radio.*]

MOSS: Bring my cigarettes when you come back, will you?

32. INTERIOR. BEDROOM

JENKINSON *switches on the radio. We hear a commentary in Italian of the start of the Mille Miglia in the Piazza Vittorio. Behind the commentators a brassband is playing, people are shouting and clapping.*

MOSS *and* JENKINSON *stand quite still and listen. The background noises of the crowd, band, etc.*

Fade away as the first car moves on to the starting ramp. It is a small car. We hear its engine rev and then, with a deafening cheer from the crowd, it drives away.

JENKINSON *looks at* MOSS *and smiles.*

JENKINSON: That's the first one. Fiat 1600. They'll be sending off the little ones in a moment — one cylinder Isottas. Forty miles an hour. I wouldn't mind when it's all over. They say the scenery is marvellous.

[JENKINSON *is now obviously relaxed and undresses for bed. From now on, at regular one minute intervals, an engine starts, revs up and then recedes in the distance.*]

MOSS: If I had to go slow I'd rather walk it.

JENKINSON: That's making yourself part of the scenery.

MOSS: That's right. Those peasants on the road.

[*They listen to the commentary.*]

MOSS: [*Another car*] Fiat.

JENKINSON: You said 'had to'.

MOSS: What?

JENKINSON: If you 'had to' go slow.

112

MOSS: So?

JENKINSON: Don't you ever want to?

MOSS: [*Already in his pyjamas, sitting on his bed*] No. If I'm
going, I want to go fast... the fastest. I've sometimes
thought about being really slow... that that's different...
those peasants. I remember one clearly. I don't know why,
an old woman. We had stopped the car somewhere and
were looking at the road surface. San Benedetto, I think.
She came past driving a donkey. That's the real
alternative, isn't it? That, or alone on a G.P. circuit in a
formula one car. No destination, using your hands, feet,
eyes, brain to balance an equation that's changing ten
times a second. Caracciolo said it once... the most
intoxicating sensation in life, or something like that. Forty
miles an hour is a compromise.

[*They listen to the commentary.*]

JENKINSON: You know something, I think I'm actually going to
sleep tonight.

MOSS: [*Smiling at him*] Feeling better?

JENKINSON: It's started. We're committed.

MOSS: To starting.

JENKINSON: Only that?

MOSS: We could funk it tomorrow. Drive at only eight-tenths.

JENKINSON: I don't think we will.

MOSS: No, of course. But what I mean is there's still time, still
ways of turning back. There are moments of no return,
but they're still coming, in the race itself. That one corner
outside Acquapendente. Remember? We've decided it's
ninety miles an hour, driving nine-tenths. I will too, if the
weather is good. I'll bring it down to just that, not a mile
an hour slower, and then go in. Then there's no way out
except the other end. No turning back, no changing our
minds. [*The commentary.* MOSS *is now in bed*] That's what
we'd like to be like, isn't it?

JENKINSON: What?

MOSS: I dunno — it's such a mess... crashing all the time. We live
it like amateurs. But put all that chaos together, pack it
into a few hours — tight! — and give a man a way
through it, clean, decisive, a reward for his talent, skill, his

113

concentration, his little bit of courage!... That's the circuit. Round and round, getting nowhere, it seems... and it does lead somewhere. Into yourself. I want to win tomorrow and that means beating Fangio, Taruffi and the others. But it's not really them I'm up against. It's myself. All I've got I'm going to bring to the moment and its decision. I'm not frightened of consequences. It should be possible to live that way — flat out — where the choices and the decisions really matter — all the time. Maybe I'd give up racing if I knew how to live like that. But I don't.

[*They listen to the commentary.*]

JENKINSON: So the game becomes life.

MOSS: What? Yes.

JENKINSON: And the rest?

[*Pause. They listen to the commentary, crowd noises.*]

MOSS: Listen to them.

JENKINSON: A hundred million lira if you draw the winner's number. Somebody's going to get 722. He'll be the only one praying for us.

MOSS: He mightn't even bother.

[*Pause.*]

JENKINSON: Heard enough?

MOSS: I think so. Good night.

JENKINSON: Good night.

TEXT:

On May the 1st, 1955, Stirling Moss, with Denis Jenkinson as his passenger and navigator, won the one thousand mile Mille Miglia... the first English driver ever to do so. Their total time for the course was ten hours, seven minutes and forty-eight seconds... an average speed of 97,8 miles an hour. This was a new record for the Mille Miglia and will stand for all time. The race was abandoned two years later as being too dangerous.

Orestes

An Experiment in Theatre as described in a Letter to an American friend

Cast

OLDER WOMAN
YOUNG WOMAN
YOUNG MAN

Dear Bruce,

When you first wrote to me (eighteen months ago?) I had every intention of sending you something which I think involves my purest statement yet in visual terms, as opposed to the literary. I finally did not do so because people who know you, your work, your America, felt that too many of the elements in what I intended sending you would not mean anything outside the context of a South African experience. Although I didn't agree with them they succeeded in making me feel insecure and so nothing happened. Your letter yesterday, however, coupled with a recent re-encounter with your work, has cut through all that nonsense.

I want to tell you about *Orestes*. Just under two years ago I was given the chance of working with three actors of my own choice with no strings attached by way of a commitment to a public performance. It was in every sense a workshop scene. For a long time I had wanted to try and make a valid theatrical experience using methods other than completed script, set rehearsal period, performance deadline, etc., etc. I was given the chance. The three actors and myself disappeared into a rehearsal room, and ten weeks later we came out and gave our first 'exposure'. The experience of those ten weeks forced us eventually to jettison a fair amount of the useless baggage we were carting around as 'theatre pros'... pseudo-terminology disguising half-truths, self-deception and vanity being among them. We stayed working on and exposing the project for another six weeks by which time money ran out and we had to disband.

At the time of the last exposure we shared with our spectators an experience which lasted about eighty minutes and which had a 'text' of about four hundred words. The rest was space, silence and action. I could write you another letter at least as long as I imagine this one is going to be, describing the methods and techniques we used, but that is not what we are on about at this point. Instead I am going to try to describe to you what the audience was witness to, what happened.

The following programme note was the only external aid to the spectator:

From Greek mythology comes the story of Clytemnestra. Her husband was Agamemnon. She had two children, Electra and Orestes. Agamemnon sacrificed their third child, Iphigenia, so that the wind would turn and the Greek fleet could leave Aulis for the Trojan War.

Agamemnon returned to Clytemnestra ten years later when she murdered him. Orestes and Electra avenged his death by killing their mother.

From our history comes the image of a young man with a large brown suitcase on a bench in the Johannesburg station concourse. He was not travelling anywhere.

For your benefit I would like to add this: for most South Africans the young man with the suitcase suggests John Harris, a twenty-six-year-old white South African. In an appalling desperate protest about the world in which he found himself, he took a suitcase full of dynamite and petrol, wired to a time fuse, into the Johannesburg Railway Station and left it beside a bench. It exploded, killing a young child and severely burning an old woman. He was caught, tried and executed.

Our spectators came into a large room with a single row of chairs around the wall. Nothing else. The three actors, already seated but as separate from each other as the circumstances would allow, were not conspicuous and could in fact have been mistaken for early spectators were it not that they were fairly well known. No lights, no costumes, no make-up and only a few small properties which you will hear about. The actors were a young man, a young woman and an older woman.

The young man, completely self-absorbed, toyed idly with an empty matchbox as the spectators came in and sat down. His manner and actions were, to start with, completely inconsequential and in no way attracted attention. The 'action' proper of the piece began when he placed the matchbox on his thigh and started pushing it toward his knee. Here again this action was of the most inconsequential order. We directed our spectators' attention to it by way of the quiet concentration of the other two actors on what the young man was doing. It never failed to work. Before the matchbox had travelled halfway to his knee — he pushed it along carefully in short little movements — our spectators were quietly attentive and expectant.

The matchbox reaches the edge of his knee. His concentration on it has become more intense. His body is hunched forward as he gives it another fractional shove with the index finger of his right hand... another... and yet another. It is now very unstable... one more touch... and it Falls! Our audience, led unobtrusively to this moment of quiet tension, relaxes visibly.

We have had our first climax, our first dramatic metaphor, namely, The Limit... that point at which something when subjected to a relentless pressure must yield, break or collapse. This metaphor was crucial to the experience which lay ahead for the audience. It was a reduction to the simplest possible terms of the experience and dilemma of Crisis.

The young man retrieved the matchbox from the floor and started to explore its other possibilities. It was empty. Pushing in and out the little drawer made noises. Tapping on it with his fingers made noises. His self-absorption, his almost total encapsulation in 'self' was very heightened simply by virtue of the fact that seventy people were witnessing it.

The next development was the discovery by this one unique centre of awareness, until now seemingly conscious only by himself, of another. With his eyes closed the young man had been making noises with his matchbox. He slowly becomes aware of a response to what he is doing and locates it aurally. It is the young woman making an almost identical sound with her tongue. From initially only concentrating on and watching the young man she has shown a progressive desire for involvement in the very simple and innocent experiences he is exploring. I should have put 'shown' in inverted commas because here again there was almost nothing tangible for you to put your finger on. It was purely a question of 'vibes'... in her case alert and eager for involvement. The moment of discovery, of finding 'another', is for me one of the absolutely elemental experiences of life. What, after all, does Heaven or Hell start and end with except the 'other'. My total absorption with the two-hander in terms of plays is simply because to this day I still stand staggered by the mysterious and unresolved equation of 'self' and 'the other'.

To return to *Orestes*. Two people, two centres of awareness, have found each other, have made contact. The matchbox and the very basic impulse to play provide the vocabulary and energy for their first encounter.

At the rate at which I am going this letter is going to be a hundred pages long (we're above five minutes into the exposure at this point!) so let me be ruthless.

Drawing closer and closer to each other, both physically and in terms of shared experience, they create for us as we watch them an adult metaphor of innocence. They play games with the matchbox. That sentence might make you squirm but do believe me that what the spectators saw was as free of sentiment, self-consciousness and pretence, as a fossil is of meat. I like that image! So much of *Orestes* was an attempt to articulate, by way of dramatic metaphor, very primitive if not archetypal experiences.

The first words were spoken by the young woman. From her first timid but hopeful approach to the young man and his matchbox, she has grown into a security of 'self'. At the climax of one of their games she says eagerly:

"Let's dream about the sea!"

The boy... because at this stage specific youthful identities have emerged out of their games, and not just as boy and girl but as self-centred boy and too-compliant girl... the boy turns his back on her suggestion and continues his involvement with his matchbox. She is for a moment self-conscious of being

120

rejected, but then decides to dream alone. (All of their games have of course been played on the floor.) Her hurt and embarrassment were seen most clearly in her relationship with the third actor, the older woman, which she created virtually out of thin air with one look, a simple 'awareness of presence'.

The older woman up until now has been a passive spectator of the games. I forgot to mention that this actress was in a sense the only conspicuous member of the trio, as her chair was placed with some prominence at the end of, but still inside, the space in which the actors worked. Passive is also not an accurate description of her role at this point. A development has taken place, from just watching to watching and enjoying and from that to caring. By virtue of their ages and the first tentative relationships in the games, the three actors are beginning to suggest 'mother and children'.

The girl moves away from the boy, nearer the older woman, and starts to dream about the sea. Here again let me be ruthless and skip the specifics... out of her action emerges the image of a child playing on a beach. Behind a front of apparent indifference, the girl slowly seduces the boy away from his games and into her dream. At first this simply involves him driving his matchbox through her sand. She, however, finally traps him permanently in her dream by smoothing a patch of sand with her feet and then looking up at the older woman and asking innocently:

"How do you spell 'Orestes'?"

The older woman spells the name slowly and simply but somehow it still manages to sound like a relic dug up out of Agamemnon's tomb at Mycenae... green and encrusted with age.

As she spells — and what can we do now except call her 'Clytemnestra' — our Electra starts to write in the smooth sand. The boy was stopped short at the mention of the name, his name. Behind an expression of primitive innocence he marvels as it slowly takes shape. After the second 'O' he joins the girl and they write alternate letters. When it is completed they sit back and look at it.

The dream continues. The girl offers the boy a handful of dry sand, but gets no response. She finds some wet sand and

121

makes a sand-bomb, showing him how it disintegrates when she strikes the hand holding it from underneath. A flicker of response this time. She makes a second bomb but something in her manner — a secret smile to the older woman — warns him in time. Before she can throw it at him he has fashioned one of his own. A marvellous sand-fight ensues. At the end of this the girl confronts the woman. We feel she wants to reach her but is afraid of the water separating them. The older woman realizes this and holds out her arms to encourage her.

Returning to this letter a day later I am convinced that what I have done so far has in fact undermined what I had hoped to do... namely, communicate some of the dramatic values which *Orestes* offered its audience. I'm sure I am fouling up the works by giving you my cerebral subtext rather than the images. Let me try to do that now as I pick up where I left off.

The boy and the girl launch out into a 'little sea' (a shallow stretch of water on the beach) in order to reach the older woman. They have enormous fun in struggling to her, but are so engrossed in their game they do not see what is happening to her. From a frank, caring and loving relationship to them she slowly turns inward to herself. By the time they reach her the process is complete. She is heavy with child. At the very moment that they arrive triumphantly at her feet, she stands up and leaves them. They watch her go... They only have each other.

The woman gets heavier and heavier. The moment arrives and Iphigenia is born. The actress in question — one of the most special performing talents I have ever encountered — created a fantastic image here. Apart from what she did with her body she took the name 'Iphigenia', broke it down into its elements — grunts, snarls, groans — and used these as her text. With great labour she put them painfully together and the name 'Iphigenia' was born.

Under the pretext that he was going to betroth the young Iphigenia to Achilles, Agamemnon lured his daughter away from his wife and down to Aulis where the Greek fleet was stranded by unfavourable winds. He sacrificed her to the

Gods. The wind turned and the Greek fleet sailed for Troy
leaving behind them a desolate Clytemnestra with the name
'Iphigenia' on her lips:

first called, as a mother would to a child in the next room...
silence
then called a little louder as if she were playing in the garden...
silence
louder still, as if she was quite far away...
silence
and still louder, shouted, screamed, whispered...
silence
then broken down again into its elementary syllables to provide
  a vocabulary for grief...
silence.
There can be no other possible response.

Time, and a chair called Agamemnon.
  I confronted the actress with a chair in the rehearsal room:
"This is unique, Y. There is not another one like it in the
world. It is useful, a 'good' thing. It will hold and cradle the
full weight of you. And because it is useful it is also beautiful.
Get to know it. Explore it until you get to know every crack in
its wood, every creak from its joints, every scab of peeling
paint. Love it. And as you love it, look for its flaw, its
imperfection, its one fatal weakness."
  The actress did all I had asked of her.
  Then:
  "Have you found the weakness? Good. Now destroy it. Start
with that small piece of torn upholstery and utterly destroy it,
using only your hands. I want to see it completely obliterated.
Given time and the discovery of the flaw you could do that to
a Sherman tank."
  Every night, every performance, that is, Clytemnestra
destroyed one unique, irreplaceable chair called Agamemnon.
It was an awesome and chilling spectacle.
  You cannot destroy without being destroyed. As she went
through the experience Y wrecked her soul. It was a devastated
human being who sank down finally into the debris, the

splintered and shattered wood, torn upholstery and padding, the bent bolts, of what had once been a good thing.

You cannot witness destruction without being damaged. The boy and girl, who had seen everything, move quietly to the remnant of an identity, the older woman, collapsed among the remnants of a chair called Agamemnon. But she does not register them. She will never see them, or anything else for that matter, properly again. They are terrified. Their metaphor of innocence has met a metaphor of evil. Nothing will ever be the same again.

But they try... they try their games in a desperate attempt to return to what they were once. But the erosion of the spirit is at work. First they lose sight. They call to each other, and like blind people find each other. There is a moment of relief, but it is illusory. They try to play together, but because they are unable to see, this is impossible. The erosion continues... one by one the possibilities, the senses that enable us to find and relate to another human being fall away. And when that process is complete, when they experience themselves individually as alone in the most terrible sense of that word, the ugliest of all transformations takes place... they become a threat to each other.

Their abortive games escalate into a nightmare at the end of which she has caught him, confined him, taking away from him even the possibility of standing erect as a man. She sits astride a savage little gaol fashioned out of chairs, singing nursery rhymes while he — mute, foetal — struggles for escape. That only happens as it can only happen in life to anyone searching for escape, searching for significant action as a response to the evil in his world, by taking on the total responsibility of being himself.

Our textual statement for this moment was when he, breaking a long silence, finally answered the following questions:

"Who are you?
What is your sex?
What is your colour?
What is your nationality?
Where are you?"

124

"Me. Male. White. South African. Here."

He is released, given a large brown suitcase and starts to walk. The girl ticks away the seconds of his life, of the bomb's life, of someone else's life, by tapping the nail of her index finger on the empty matchbox.

The bench in a station concourse. An old woman rises from the debris of an act of destruction. Her first line, hollow with regret and loneliness, is unbearably poignant:

"I want to go back now."

She shuffles toward the bench half-singing barely audible snatches from 'White Cliffs of Dover', 'Ferry Boat Serenade', 'Begin the Beguine'... echoes of other times, good times, and other places, now far away. A young woman also arrives at the bench, and finally a young man with a suitcase.

They drift around it, encountering each other in a slow somnambulistic ritual of finding and losing, of fearing and of sad and foredoomed attempts at trying to reach each other. The older woman is haunted by the ghost of a little girl, of a small, sweaty, little hand that she finds unexpectedly in hers, only to lose it just as unexpectedly.

After what seems an eternity of nothing happening, of non-relating, the young man sits down and opens his suitcase. It is full of newspapers. He fashions round bombs as he was taught once, long ago in a game on a beach. The old woman is beside him. He places a bomb in each of her hands. She thinks he wants to play. She also has a memory, but much, much dimmer than his, of a game on a beach. Something like a smile moves across her face.

But then the bombs go off.

The moment is presented to us in slow, very slow motion.

Her head goes back slowly and she makes noises suggestive of pain as her feet come up, the toes crimped in. The feet rise still higher, the head goes back still further and the hands drop their paper bombs. We barely hear her say:

"How am I going to walk?"

She pushes herself to the edge of the bench and drops to the floor. She experiences herself as being utterly alone. The petrol has burnt away the soles of her feet. She wants to walk but cannot. She wants to cry but all that comes out are small sounds of disgust as she grabs her ankles and, using her heels and her arse, drags herself away across the floor of a station concourse so vast and empty it looks like the floor of a palace. There is torn paper everywhere.

After a pause, the actors relax, return to the bench and read the following texts:

YOUNG MAN [from the testimony of John Harris]: I felt, terrifically, ecstatically happy while sitting on the bench. The suitcase was on the right of me in the shelter above Platforms Five and Six. I knew that what I was doing was right. Later I heard that people had been hurt, but this did not make sense because I had known that people were not going to be hurt.

YOUNG WOMAN [from R.D. Laing's *The Divided Self*]: Some people go through life with vomit on their lips. You can feel their terrible hunger but they defy you to feed them. It's hellish misery to see the breast being offered gladly and with love, but to know that getting close to it will make you hate it, the way you hated your mother. I wanted to tear out my stomach for being so hungry.

OLDER WOMAN [from R.D. Laing's *The Bird of Paradise*]: If I could turn you on, if I could drive you out of your wretched mind, if I could tell you, I would let you know.

These texts had been the actors' major provocations during our rehearsal period. In addition to Laing's writing and John Harris's testimony, another major provocation in our work came from Grotowski's book of essays, *Towards a Poor Theatre*.

Yrs
Athol Fugard

The Drummer

Cast

AN ACTOR

Note: I only saw him once, but that was enough. His immediate identity was that of a bum ... what looked like an old army overcoat with a bit of rope serving as a belt and a head of wild, unwashed and uncombed hair. I remember one seemingly incongruous detail — a length of bright yellow material, tied around his neck, which he wore like a cape.

It was a very busy hour in Times Square, New York, and he was moving effortlessly through the congested traffic beating out a tattoo with a pair of drumsticks on anything that came to hand. In the half hour or so that I followed him he dealt in this fashion with a series of manholes in the street, passing motorcar bonnets, lampposts on the pavement and one mail box. He wasn't begging. In fact in his relationship to the world around him the roles of giver and receiver seemed to be just the reverse. He was very joyous ... defiantly so! ... and seemed to have a sense of himself as being extravagantly free.

A pile of rubbish on a pavement, waiting to be cleared away. This consists of an over-filled trash-can and a battered old chair with torn upholstery on which is piled an assortment of cardboard boxes and plastic bags full of discarded junk.

Distant and intermittent city noises. These will increase in volume and frequency as the action demands.

A bum enters. He walks over to the pile of rubbish and starts to work his way through it ... looking for something useful in terms of that day's survival. He has obviously just woken up and yawns from time to time. After a few seconds he clears the chair, sits down, makes himself comfortable and continues his search.

One of the boxes produces a drumstick. He examines it and then abandons it.

129

A little later he finds a second drumstick. He examines it.
Remembers! He scratches around in the pile of rubbish at his
feet and retrieves the first.

Two drumsticks! His find intrigues him.

Another dip into the rubbish but it produces nothing further
of interest.

Two drumsticks!

He settles back in his chair and surveys the world.

An ambulance siren approaches and recedes stage right.

He observes indifferently.

A fire engine approaches and recedes stage left.

He observes.

While this is going on he taps idly on the lid of the trash-can
with one of the drumsticks.

He becomes aware of this little action.

Two drumsticks and a trash-can!

It takes him a few seconds to realize the potential.

He straightens up in his chair and with a measure of
caution, attempts a little tattoo on the lid of the can.

The result is not very impressive.

He makes a second attempt, with the same result.

Problem.

Solution!

He gets up and empties the trash-can of its contents,
replaces the lid and makes a third attempt.

The combination of a serious intention and the now-
resonant bin produces a decided effect.

He develops it and in so doing starts to enjoy himself.

His excitement gets him on to his feet.

He has one last flash of inspiration.

He removes the lid from the can, up-ends it, and with great
bravura drums out a final tattoo... virtually an
accompaniment to the now very loud and urgent city noises all
around him.

Embellishing his appearance with some item from the
rubbish... a cape?... and holding his drumsticks at the ready
he chooses a direction and sets off to take on the city.

He has discovered it is full of drums... and he has got
drumsticks.

My Children! My Africa!

For Lisa and for John

Characters

MR M'S full name: Anela Myalatya. Principal of the Zolile High
   School. In his early fifties. A bachelor. Bespectacled and
   passionate about his vocation as a teacher.
ISABEL DYSON, matric class of the Camdeboo Girls High School.
   Eighteen years old. Strong, forceful personality with a
   sharp, enquiring mind. A refreshing sense of humour.
   Loves winning, hates losing.
THAMI MBIKWANA, matric class of the Zolile High School.
   Nineteen years old. Behind a reserved and soft spoken
   manner, a strong personality with a sly sense of humour.
   He is also very bright. Mr M describes him, accurately, as
   a born leader.

The action of the play takes place in a small Eastern Cape
Karoo town in the autumn of 1984.

My Children! My Africa premièred on 27th June 1989, at the
Market Theatre, Johannesburg, presented by The Company.
The production was directed by Athol Fugard, designed by
Susan Hilferty, with lighting by Mannie Manim and sound by
Patrick Curtis. John Kani played Mr M, with Kathy-Jo Ross
as Isabel and Rapulana Seiphemo as Thami.

ACT ONE

SCENE 1

Classroom of the Zolile High School.
MR M *is at a table with* THAMI *and* ISABEL *on either side of him.*
A lively inter-school debate is in progress. Everybody is speaking
at the same time.
MR M: Order please!
ISABEL: I never said anything of the kind.
THAMI: Yes you did. You said that women were more...
MR M: I call you both to order!
ISABEL: What I said was that women...
THAMI: ... were more emotional than men...
ISABEL: Correction! That woman were more intuitive than
    men...
MR M: Miss Dyson and Mr Mbikwana! Will you both please...
ISABEL: You are twisting my words and misquoting me.
THAMI: I am not. I am simply asking you...
MR M: Come to order! [*Grabs the school bell and rings it violently.*
    It works. Silence]
    I think it is necessary for me to remind all of you exactly
    what a debate is supposed to be. [*Opens and reads from*
    little black dictionary that is at hand on the table] My
    dictionary defines it as follows: 'The orderly and regulated
    discussion of an issue with opposing viewpoints receiving
    equal time and consideration.' Shouting down the
    opposition so that they cannot be heard does not comply
    with that definition.
    Enthusiasm for your cause is most commendable but

135

without personal discipline it is as useless as having a good donkey and a good cart but no harness.

We are now running out of time. I am therefore closing the open section of our debate. No more interruptions from the floor, please. We'll bring our proceedings to a close with a brief, I repeat *brief*, three minutes at the most, summing up of our arguments.

Starting with the proposers of the motion: Mr Thami Mbikwana of the Zolile High School, will you please make your concluding statement.

[THAMI *stands up. Wild round of applause from the audience. He is secure and at ease... he is speaking to an audience of schoolmates. His 'concluding statement' is outrageous and he knows it and enjoys it.*]

THAMI: I don't stand here now and speak to you as your friend and schoolmate. That would lessen the seriousness of my final words to you. No! Close your eyes, forget that you know my face and voice, forget that you know anything about Thami Mbikwana. Think of me rather as an oracle, of my words as those of the great ancestors of our traditional African culture which we turn our back on and desert to our great peril!

The opposition has spoken about sexual exploitation and the need for women's liberation. Brothers and sisters, these are foreign ideas. Do not listen to them. They come from a culture, the so-called Western Civilisation, that has meant only misery to Africa and its people. It is the same culture that shipped away thousands of our ancestors as slaves, the same culture that has exploited Africa with the greed of a vulture during the period of Colonialism and the same culture which continues to exploit us in the twentieth century under the disguise of concern for our future.

The opposition has not been able to refute my claim that women cannot do the same jobs as men because they are not equals of us physically and that a woman's role in the family, in society, is totally different to that of the man's. These facts taken together reinforce what our fathers, and our grandfathers and our great-grandfathers knew —

136

namely, that happiness and prosperity for the tribe and the nation is achieved when education of the little ladies takes these facts into consideration. Would it be right for a woman to go to war while a man sits at the sewing machine? I do not have milk in my breasts to feed the baby while my wife is out digging up roads for the Divisional Council. [*Wild laughter*] Brothers and sisters, it is obvious that you feel the same as I do about this most serious matter. I hope that at the end of this debate, your vote will reflect your agreement with me.

[*Wild applause and whistles.*]

MR M: Thank you, Mr Mbikwana. [THAMI *sits*] And now finally, a last statement from the captain of the visiting team, Miss Isabel Dyson of Camdeboo Girls High.

[*Polite applause.* ISABEL *stands. She takes on the audience with direct unflinching eye contact. She is determined not to be intimidated.*]

ISABEL: You have had to listen to a lot of talk this afternoon about traditional values, traditional society, your great ancestors, your glorious past. In spite of what has been implied I want to start off by telling you that I have as much respect and admiration for your history and tradition as anybody else. I believe most strongly that there are values and principles in traditional African society which could be studied with great profit by the Western Civilisation so scornfully rejected by the previous speaker. But at the same time, I know, and you know, that Africa no longer lives in that past. For better or for worse it is part now of the twentieth century and all the nations on this continent are struggling very hard to come to terms with that reality. Arguments about sacred traditional values, the traditional way of life, et cetera and et cetera, are used by those who would like to hold back Africa's progress and keep it locked up in the past.

Maybe there was a time in the past when a woman's life consisted of bearing children and hoeing the fields while men sharpened their spears and sat around waiting for another war to start. But it is a silly argument that relies on that old image of primitive Africa for its strength. It is

137

an argument that insults your intelligence. Times have changed. Sheer brute strength is not the determining factor any more. You do not need the muscles of a prize-fighter when you sit down to operate the computers that control today's world. The American space programme now has women astronauts on board the space shuttles doing the same jobs as men. As for the difference in the emotional and intellectual qualities of men and women, remember that it is a question of difference and not inferiority, and that with those differences go strengths which compensate for weaknesses in the opposite sex.

And lastly, a word of warning. The argument against equality for women, in education or any other field, based on alleged 'differences' between the two sexes, is an argument that can very easily be used against any other 'different' group. It is an argument based on prejudice, not fact. I ask you not to give it your support. Thank you.

[*She sits. Polite applause.*]

MR M: Thank you, Miss Dyson. We come now to the vote. But before we do that, a word of caution. We have had a wonderful experience this afternoon. Don't let it end on a frivolous and irresponsible note. Serious issues have been debated. Vote accordingly. To borrow a phrase from Mr Mbikwana, forget the faces, remember the words. If you believe that we have the right to vote out there in the big world, then show it here in the classroom, that you know how to use it.

We'll take it on a count of hands, and for the benefit of any over-enthusiastic supporters, only one hand per person, please. Let me read the proposal once again: 'That in view of the essential physical and psychological differences between men and women, there should be correspondingly different educational syllabuses for the two sexes.'

All those in favour raise a hand. [MR M, THAMI *and* ISABEL *count hands*] Seventeen? [THAMI *and* ISABEL *nod agreement*] All those against? [*They all count again*] Twenty-four? [*Reactions from* THAMI *and* ISABEL] The proposal is defeated by twenty-four votes to seventeen. Before we break just a reminder about the special choir practice this afternoon. Members of the choir must please join Mrs Magada in Number Two Classroom after school.

[*To* ISABEL *and* THAMI] Allow me to offer my congratulations, Miss Dyson, on a most well-deserved victory. What do you say, Mbikwana?

THAMI: [*To* ISABEL] Your concluding statement was a knockout.

MR M: You didn't do too badly yourself.

ISABEL: You made me so angry!

THAMI: [*All innocence*] I did?

ISABEL: Ja you did. [THAMI *laughs.*] I was beginning to think you actually believed in what you were saying.

THAMI: But I do!

ISABEL: Oh, come on ...!

MR M: [*Rubbing his hands with pleasure*] All I can say is ... Splendid! Splendid! Splendid! The intellect in action. Challenge and response. That is what a good debate is all about. And whatever you do, young lady, don't underestimate your achievement in winning the popular vote. It wasn't easy for that audience to vote against Mbikwana. He's one of them, and a very popular 'one of them', I might add. [*Wagging a finger at* THAMI] You were quite shameless in the way you tried to exploit that loyalty.

THAMI: [*Another laugh*] Was that wrong?

MR M: No. As the saying goes, all is fair in love, war and debating. But the fact that you didn't succeed is what makes me really happy. I am very proud of our audience. In my humble opinion they are the real winners this afternoon. You two just had to talk and argue. Anybody can do that. They had to listen ... intelligently!

ISABEL: Well, all I know is that I had a good time.

MR M: That was very apparent, if I may say so, Miss Dyson. I can't thank you enough for coming to us today. I sincerely hope there'll be another occasion.

ISABEL: Same here.

MR M: Good! [*Consults his watch*] Now you must excuse me. There is a staff meeting waiting for me. Will you look after Miss Dyson, please, Mbikwana?

THAMI: Yes, teacher.

[MR M *leaves*. ISABEL *and* THAMI *pack away into their school cases the papers and books they used in the debate. Without the mediating presence of* MR M, *they are both a little self-conscious. First moves in the ensuing conversations are awkward.*]

ISABEL: I wish we had a teacher like... [*Pronouncing the name carefully*] Mr M ya lat ya. Did I say it right?

THAMI: Yes you did, but nobody calls him that. He's just plain Mr M to everybody.

ISABEL: Mr M.

THAMI: That's right.

ISABEL: Well I think he's wonderful.

THAMI: He's okay.

ISABEL: I had a geography teacher in standard seven who was a little bit like him. Full of fun and lots of energy.

THAMI: Ja, that's Mr M all right.

[*Pause.*]

ISABEL: I meant what I said to him. I really did have a good time.

THAMI: Same here.

ISABEL: You did? Because to be honest with you, I wasn't expecting it.

THAMI: Me neither.

ISABEL: No?

THAMI: Nope.

ISABEL: Why not?

THAMI: [*Embarrassed*] Well... you know...

ISABEL: Let me guess. You've never debated with girls before. [*He nods, smiling sheepishly*] And white girls at that! I don't believe it. You boys are all the same.

THAMI: But you were good!

ISABEL: Because I happen to feel very strongly about what we were debating. But it was also the whole atmosphere, you know. It was so... so free and easy. The debates at my school are such stuffy affairs. And so boring most of the time. Everything is done according to the rules with everybody being polite and nobody getting excited... lots of discipline but very little enthusiasm. This one was a riot!

140

THAMI: [*Finger to his lips*] Be careful.

ISABEL: Of what?

THAMI: That word.

ISABEL: Which one?

THAMI: Riot! Don't say it in a black township. Police start shooting as soon as they hear it.

ISABEL: Oh...

THAMI: [*Having a good laugh*] I'm sorry. It's a joke, Isabel.

ISABEL: Oh... you caught me off guard. I didn't think you would joke about those things.

THAMI: Riots and police? Oh yes, we joke about them. We joke about everything.

ISABEL: Okay, then I'll say it again. This afternoon was a riot.

THAMI: Good! Try that one on your folks when you get home tonight. Say the newspapers have got it all wrong. You had a wonderful time taking part in a little township riot. [*This time* ISABEL *does get the joke. A good laugh.*]

ISABEL: Oh ja, I can just see my Mom and Dad cracking up at that one.

THAMI: They wouldn't think it was funny? [*The subject of white reaction to location humour amuses him enormously.*]

ISABEL: Are you kidding? They even take the Marx Brothers seriously. I can just hear my Mom: "Isabel, I think it is very wrong to joke about those things!"

THAMI: Dyson! That's an English name.

ISABEL: Sober, sensible, English-speaking South African. I'm the third generation.

THAMI: What does your Dad do?

ISABEL: He's a chemist. The chemist shop in town. Karoo Pharmacy. That's ours. My mother and sister work in it as well, and on Saturdays, provided there isn't a hockey match, so do I.

THAMI: Any brothers?

ISABEL: No. Just the four of us.

THAMI: A happy family.

ISABEL: Ja, I suppose you could call us that. Mind you, Lucille would say it would be a lot happier if only her little sister would be, as she puts it, 'more accommodating of others'.

THAMI: What does she mean?

ISABEL: She means she doesn't like the fact that I've got opinions of my own. I'm the rebel in the family.

THAMI: That sounds interesting.

ISABEL: I can't help it. Whenever it's time for a family indaba ... you know, when we sit down in the lounge to discuss family business and things ... I just always seem to end up disagreeing with everybody and wanting to do things differently. But other than that, ja, an average sort of happy family.

What else do you want to know? Go ahead, anything ... provided I also get a turn to ask questions. [THAMI *studies her*] Eighteen years old. I think I want to be a writer. My favourite subject is English and my favourite sport, as you might have guessed, is hockey. Anything else?

THAMI: Yes. What did you have for breakfast this morning? [ISABEL *laughs.*]

ISABEL: Auntie, our maid, put down in front of me a plate of steaming, delicious Jungle Oats over which I sprinkled a crust of golden, brown sugar, and while that was melting on top I added a little moat of chilled milk all around the side. That was followed by brown-bread toast, quince jam and lots and lots of tea.

THAMI: Yes, you're a writer.

ISABEL: You think so?

THAMI: You made me hungry.

ISABEL: My turn now?

THAMI: Yep.

ISABEL: Let's start with your family.

THAMI: Mbikwana! [*He clears his throat.*] Mbikwana is an old Bantu name and my mother and my father are good, reliable, ordinary, hard-working Bantu-speaking black South African natives. I am the one hundred thousandth generation.

ISABEL: You really like teasing, don't you?

THAMI: Amos and Lilian Mbikwana. They're in Cape Town. My mother is a domestic and my father works for the railways. I stay here with my grandmother and married sister. I was sent to school here in the peaceful platteland because it is so much safer, you see, than the big city with

142

all its temptations and troubles. [THAMI *laughs*] Another
Bantu joke.

ISABEL: You're impossible!

[*They are now beginning to relax with each other.* ISABEL
finds the class register on the desk.]

ISABEL: Zolile High School. Standard Ten. [*She opens it and
reads*] Awu.

THAMI: [*Pointing to the appropriate desk in the classroom*] There.

ISABEL: Bandla.

THAMI: There.

ISABEL: Cwati.

THAMI: Cwati. There.

ISABEL: Who was the chap sitting there who laughed at *all* your
jokes and applauded *everything* you said?

THAMI: Stephen Gaika. He's mad.

ISABEL: And your best friend?

THAMI: They are all my friends.

ISABEL: And where does... [*She finds his name in the register.*]
Thami Mbikwana sit?

[THAMI *points.* ISABEL *goes to the desk and sits.*]

THAMI: Yes, that's the one. For nearly two years I've sat there...
being educated!

ISABEL: [*Reading names carved into the wood of the desk*] John,
Bobby, Zola, Bo... Boni...

THAMI: Bonisile.

ISABEL: Where's your name?

THAMI: You won't find it there. I don't want to leave any part of
me in this classroom.

ISABEL: That sound's heavy.

THAMI: It's been heavy. You got no problems with it, hey?

ISABEL: With school! No. Not really. Couple of teachers have
tried their best to spoil it for me, but they haven't
succeeded. I've had a pretty good time, in fact. I think I
might even end up with the old cliché... you know, school
years, best years, happiest years... Whatever it is they say.

THAMI: No. I won't be saying that.

ISABEL: That surprises me.

THAMI: Why?

ISABEL: Ja, come on, so would you be if I said it. You're obviously

143

clever. I bet you sail through your exams.

THAMI: It's not as simple as just passing exams, Isabel. School doesn't mean the same to us that it does to you.

ISABEL: Go on.

THAMI: I used to like it. Junior school? You should have seen me. I wanted them to have school on Saturdays and Sundays as well. Yes, I did. Other boys wanted to kill me. I hated the holidays.

ISABEL: So what changed?

THAMI: I changed.

ISABEL: Ja, I'm listening.

THAMI: [*A shrug*] That's all. I changed. Things changed. Everything changed.

ISABEL: [*Realising she is not going to get more out of him*] Only five months to go.

THAMI: I'm counting.

ISABEL: What then?

THAMI: After school? [*Another shrug*] I don't know yet. Do you?

ISABEL: Ja. Rhodes University. I want to study journalism.

THAMI: Newspaper reporter.

ISABEL: And radio, TV. It's a very wide field now. You can specialise in all sorts of things. [*Perplexed*] Don't you want to study further, Thami?

THAMI: I told you, I'm not sure about anything yet.

ISABEL: What does Mr M say?

THAMI: It's got nothing to do with him.

ISABEL: But you're his favourite, aren't you? [*Non-committal shrug from* THAMI] I bet you are. And I also bet you anything you like that he's got a career planned out for you.

THAMI: [*Sharply*] What I do with my life has got nothing to do with him.

ISABEL: Sorry.

THAMI: I don't listen to what he says and I don't do what he says.

ISABEL: I said I'm sorry. I didn't mean to interfere.

THAMI: That's all right. It's just that he makes me so mad sometimes. He always thinks *he* knows what is best for me. He never tries to ask me how I feel about things. I know he means well, but I'm not a child any more. I've

144

got ideas of my own now.

ISABEL: [*Placating*] Ja, I know what you mean. I've had them in
my life as well. They always know what is best for you,
don't they? So anyway, listen... I'm going to write up the
debate for our school newspaper. I'll send you a copy if
you like.

THAMI: You got a school newspaper! How about that!

ISABEL: It's a bit unethical reporting on a contest in which I took
part, and won, but I promise to be objective. I made notes
of most of your main points.

THAMI: You can have my speech if you want it.

ISABEL: Hell, thanks. That will make it much easier... and
guarantee there won't be any misquotes!

[THAMI *hands over the speech. It is obvious that they both
want to prolong the conversation, but this is prevented by the
sound of* MR M'S *bell being rung vigorously in the distance.
They check wristwatches.*]

ISABEL: Oh my God, look at the time!

[*They grab their school cases and run.*]

SCENE 2

ISABEL *alone.*
She speaks directly to the audience.

ISABEL: It's on the edge of town, on the right hand side when you
drive out to join the National Road going north to
Middelburg. Unfortunately, as most of Camdeboo would
say, you can't miss it. I discovered the other day that it
has actually got a name... Brakwater... from the old
farm that used to be there. Now everybody just calls it 'the
location'. There's been a lot of talk lately about moving it
to where it can't be seen. Our mayor, Mr Pienaar, was in
our shop the other day and I heard him say to my Dad
that it was "very much to be regretted" that the first thing
that greeted any visitor to the town was the "terrible mess
of the location". To be fair to old Pienaar he has got a
point you know. Our town is very pretty. We've got a lot

145

of nicely restored National Monument houses and buildings. Specially in the Main Street. Our shop is one of them. The location is quite an eyesore by comparison. Most of the houses — if you can call them that — are made of bits of old corrugated iron or anything else they could find to make four walls and a roof. There are no gardens or anything like that. You've got to drive in first gear all the time because of the potholes and stones, and when the wind is blowing and all the dust and rubbish flying around...! I think you'd be inclined to agree with our mayor.

I've actually been into it quite a few times. With my Mom to visit Auntie, our maid, when she was sick. And with my Dad when he had to take emergency medicine to the clinic. I can remember one visit, just sitting in the car and staring out of the window trying to imagine what it would be like to live my whole life in one of those little pondoks. No electricity, no running water. No privacy! Auntie's little house has only got two small rooms and nine of them sleep there. I ended up being damn glad I was born with a white skin.

But don't get the wrong idea. I'm not saying I've spent a lot of time thinking about it seriously or anything like that.

It's just been there, you know, on the edge of my life, the way it is out there on the edge of town. So when Miss Brockway, our principal, called me in and told me that the black school had started a debating society and had invited us over for a debate, I didn't have any objections. She said it was a chance for a "pioneering intellectual exchange" between the two schools.

She also said she had checked with the police and they had said it would be all right provided we were driven straight to the school and then straight out afterwards. There's been a bit of trouble in the location again and people are starting to get nervous about it. So off we went... myself, Renee Vermaas and Cathy Bullard, the C.G.H. Debating Team... feeling very virtuous about our 'pioneering' mission in the location. As Renee tactfully put it: "Shame!

146

We must remember that English isn't their home language. So don't use too many big words and speak slowly and carefully."

They were waiting for us in what they called Number One Classroom. [*Shaking her head*] Honestly, I would rate it as the most bleak, depressing, dingy classroom I have ever been in. Everything about it was grey — the cement floor, the walls, the ceiling. When I first saw it, I thought to myself, how in God's name does anybody study or learn anything in here. But there they were, about forty of them, my age, mostly boys, not one welcoming smile among the lot of them. And they *were* studying something and very intently... three privileged and uncomfortable white girls, in smart uniforms, from a posh school, who had come to give them a lesson in debating. I know I'm a good debater and one of the reasons for that is that I always talk very directly to the audience and the opposition. I am not shy about making eye contact. Well, when I did it this time, when it was my turn to speak and I stood up and looked at those forty unsmiling faces, I suddenly realised that I hadn't prepared myself for one simple but all-important fact: they had no intention of being grateful to me. They were sitting there waiting to judge me, what I said and how I said it, on the basis of total equality. Maybe it doesn't sound like such a big thing to you, but you must understand I had never really confronted that before, and I don't just mean in debates. I mean in my life!

I'm not saying I've had no contact across the colour line. Good heavens, no! I get as much of that as any average young white South African. I have a great time every morning with Auntie in the kitchen when she's cooking breakfast and we gossip about everything and everybody in town. And then there's Samuel with his crash helmet and scooter... he delivers medicine for my Dad... I have wonderful long conversations with him about religion and the meaning of life generally. He's a very staunch Zionist. Church every Sunday. But it's always 'Miss Isabel', the baas's daughter, that he's talking to. When I stood up in front of those black matric pupils in Number One

Classroom it was a very different story. I wasn't at home
or in my Dad's shop or in my school or any of the other
safe places in my life.

I was in Brakwater! It was *their* school. It was *their* world.
I was the outsider and I was being asked to prove myself.
Standing there in front of them like that I felt ...
exposed! ... in a way that has never happened to me
before. Cathy told me afterwards that she's never heard
me start a debate *so* badly and finish it *so* strongly.

God, it was good! I don't know when exactly it happened,
but about half-way through my opening address, I realised
that everything about that moment ... the miserable little
classroom, myself, my voice, what I was saying and them
hearing and understanding me, because I knew they
understood me ... they were staring and listening so hard I
could feel it on my skin! ... all of it had become one of the
most real experiences I have ever had. I have never before
had so ... so exciting! ... a sense of myself. Because that *is*
what we all want, isn't it? For things to be real, our lives,
our thoughts, what we say and do? That's what I want,
now. I didn't really know it before that debate, but I do
now. You see, I finally worked out what happened to me
in the classroom. I discovered a new world! I've always
thought about the location as just a sort of embarrassing
backyard to our neat and proper little white world, where
our maids and our gardeners and our delivery boys went
at the end of the day. But it's not. It's a whole world of its
own with its own life that has nothing to do with us. If
you put together all the Brakwaters in the country, then
it's a pretty big one ... and if you'll excuse my language ...
there's a hell of a lot of people living in it! That's quite a
discovery you know. But it's also a little ... what's the
word? ... disconcerting! You see, it means that what I
thought was out there for me ...

No, it's worse than that! It's what I was made to believe
was out there for me ... the ideas, the chances, the
people ... specially the people! ... all of that is only a
small fraction of what it could be. [*Shaking her head*] No.
Or as Auntie says in the kitchen when she's not happy

148

about something... Aikona! Not good enough. I'm
greedy. I want more. I want as much as I can get.

ISABEL *alone.*
MR M *enters, hat in hand, mopping his brow with a handkerchief.*
MR M: Miss Dyson! There you are.
ISABEL: [*Surprised*] Hello!
MR M: My apologies for descending on you out of the blue like
    this, but I've been looking for you high and low. One of
    your schoolmates said I would find you here.
ISABEL: Don't apologise. It's a pleasure to see you again, Mr M.
MR M: [*Delighted*] Mr M! How wonderful to hear you call me that.
ISABEL: You must blame Thami for my familiarity.
MR M: Blame him? On the contrary, I will thank him most
    gratefully. Hearing you call me Mr M like all the others at
    my school gives me the happy feeling that you are also a
    member of my very extended family.
ISABEL: I'd like to be.
MR M: Then welcome to the family, Miss...
ISABEL: [*Before he can say it*] Isabel, if you please Mr M, just
    plain Isabel.
MR M: [*Bowing*] Then doubly welcome, young Isabel.
ISABEL: [*Curtsy*] I thank you, kind sir.
MR M: You have great charm, young lady. I can understand now
    how you managed to leave so many friends behind you
    after only one visit to the school. Hardly a day passes
    without someone stopping me and asking: When is Isabel
    Dyson and her team coming back?
ISABEL: Well? When are we?
MR M: You would still welcome a return visit?
ISABEL: But of course.
MR M: Why so emphatically 'of course'?
ISABEL: Because I enjoyed the first one so emphatically very
    much.
MR M: The unruly behaviour of my young family wasn't too much
    for you?

ISABEL: Didn't I also get a little unruly once or twice, Mr M?

MR M: Yes, now that you mention it. You certainly gave as good as you got.

ISABEL: [*With relish*] And that is precisely why I enjoyed myself.

MR M: You like a good fight.

ISABEL: Ja. Specially the ones I win!

MR M: Splendid! Splendid! Splendid! Because that is precisely what I have come to offer you.

ISABEL: Your Thami wants a return bout, does he?

MR M: He will certainly welcome the opportunity to salvage his pride when it comes along... his friends are teasing him mercilessly... but what I have come to talk to you about is a prospect even more exciting than that. I have just seen Miss Brockway and she has given it her official blessing. It was her suggestion that I approach you directly. So here I am. Can you spare a few minutes?

ISABEL: As many as you like.

MR M: It came to me as I sat there in Number One trying to be an impartial referee while you and Thami went for each other hammer and tongs, no holds barred and no quarter given or asked. I don't blame our audience for being so unruly. Once or twice I felt like doing some shouting myself. What a contest! But at the same time, what a waste, I thought! Yes, you heard me correctly! A waste! They shouldn't be fighting each other. They should be fighting together! If the sight of them as opponents is so exciting, imagine what it would be like if they were allies. If those two stood side by side, if they joined forces, they could take on anybody... and win! For the next few days that is all I could think of. It tormented me. When I wrote my report about the debate in the school diary, that was the last sentence. "But oh! what a waste!"

The truth is I've seen too much of it, Isabel. Wasted people! Wasted chances! It's become a phobia with me now. It's not easy, you know, being a teacher, to put your heart and soul into educating an eager, young mind, which you know will never get a chance to develop further and realise its full potential. The thought that you and Thami would be another two victims of this country's lunacy was

150

almost too much for me. The time for lamentations is passed.

[*Envelope from his pocket*] Two days ago I received this in the mail. It's the programme for this year's Grahamstown Schools Festival. It has given me what I was looking for . . . an opportunity to fight the lunacy. The Standard Bank is sponsoring a new event: an inter-school English literature quiz. Each team to consist of two members. I'll come straight to the point. I have suggested to Miss Brockway that Zolile High and Camdeboo High join forces and enter a combined team. As I have already told you, she has agreed and so has the Festival director who I spoke to on the telephone this morning. There you have it, Isabel Dyson. I anxiously await your response.

ISABEL: I'm in the team?

MR M: Yes.

ISABEL: And . . . [*Her eyes bright with anticipation*]

MR M: That's right.

ISABEL: Thami!

MR M: Correct.

ISABEL: Mr M, you're a genius!

MR M: [*Holding up a hand to stop what was obviously going to be a very enthusiastic response*] Wait! Wait! Before you get carried away and say yes, let me warn you about a few things. It's going to mean a lot of very hard work. I am appointing myself team coach and, as Thami will tell you, I can be a very hard taskmaster. You'll have to give up a lot of free time, young lady.

ISABEL: Anything else?

MR M: Not for the moment.

ISABEL: Then I'll say it again. Mr M, you're a genius! [*Her joy is enormous, and she shows it.*] How's that for unruly behaviour?

MR M: The very worst! They couldn't do it better on the location's streets. What a heartwarming response, Isabel.

ISABEL: What were you expecting? That I would say no?

MR M: I didn't know what to expect. I knew that you would give me a sympathetic hearing, but that I would be swept off my feet, literally and figuratively . . . No. I was most certainly not prepared for that. Does my silly little idea really mean that much to you?

ISABEL: None of that, Mr M! It's not silly and it's not little and you know it.

MR M: All right. But does it really mean that much to you?

ISABEL: Yes it does.

MR M: [*Persistent*] But why?

ISABEL: The visit to Zolile was one of the best things that has happened to me. I don't want it to just end there. One visit and that's it. [MR M *listens quietly, attentively, an invitation to* ISABEL *to say more*] It feels like it could be the beginning of something. I've met you and Thami and all the others and would like to get to know you all better. But how do I do that? I can't just go after you chaps like... well, you know what I mean. Roll up and knock on your doors like you were neighbours or just living down the street. It's not as easy as that with us, is it? You're in the location, I'm in the town... and all the rest of it. So there I was feeling more and more frustrated about it all when along you come with your 'silly little' idea. It's perfect! Do I make sense?

MR M: Most definitely. Make some more.

ISABEL: I've been thinking about it, you see. When I told my Mom and Dad about the debate and what a good time I'd had, I could see they didn't really understand what I was talking about. Specially my Mom. I ended up getting very impatient with her which wasn't very smart of me because the harder I tried to make her understand the more nervous she got. Anyway, I've cooled off now and I realise why she was like that. Being with black people on an equal footing, you know... as equals, because that is how I ended up feeling with Thami and his friends... that was something that had never happened to her. She didn't know what I was talking about. And because she knows nothing about it, she's frightened of it.

MR M: You are not.

ISABEL: No. Not any more.

MR M: So you were.

ISABEL: Well, not so much frightened as sort of uncertain. You

152

see, I thought I knew what to expect, but after a few
minutes in Number One classroom I realised I was wrong
by a mile.

MR M: What had you expected, Isabel?

ISABEL: You know, that everybody would be nice and polite and
very, very grateful.

MR M: And we weren't?

ISABEL: You were, but not them. Thami and his friends. [*She
laughs at the memory.*] Ja, to be honest Mr M, that family
of yours *was* a bit scary at first. But not any more! I feel
I've made friends with Thami and the others, so now it's
different.

MR M: Simple as that.

ISABEL: Simple as that.

MR M: Knowledge has banished fear! Bravo. Bravo. And yet again
Bravo! If you knew what it meant to me to hear you speak
like that. I wasn't wrong. From the moment I first shook
hands with you I knew you were a kindred spirit.

ISABEL: Tell me more about the competition.

MR M: First prize is five thousand rand which the bank has
stipulated must be spent on books for the school library.
We will obviously divide it equally between Camdeboo
and Zolile when you and Thami win.

ISABEL: Yes, what about my team-mate? What does he say? Have
you asked him yet?

MR M: No, I haven't *asked* him Isabel, and I won't. I will *tell* him,
and when I do I trust he will express as much enthusiasm
for the idea as you have. I am an old-fashioned
traditionalist in most things, young lady, and my
classroom is certainly no exception. I teach, Thami learns.
He understands and accepts that that is the way it should
be. You don't like the sound of that, do you?

ISABEL: Does sound a bit dictatorial, you know.

MR M: It might sound that way but I assure you it isn't. We do not
blur the difference between the generations in the way that
you white people do. Respect for authority, right
authority, is deeply ingrained in the African soul. It's all
I've got when I stand there in Number One. Respect for
my authority is my only teaching aid. If I ever lost it those

153

young people will abandon their desks and take to the streets. I expect Thami to trust my judgement of what is best for him, and he does. That trust is the most sacred responsibility in my life.

ISABEL: He's your favourite, isn't he?

MR M: Good heavens! A good teacher doesn't have favourites! Are you suggesting that I might be a bad one? Because if you are... [*Looking around*] you would be right, young lady. Measured by that yardstick I am a very bad teacher indeed. He *is* my favourite. Thami Mbikwana! Yes, I have waited for a long time for him. To tell you the truth I had given up all hope of him ever coming along. Any teacher who takes his calling seriously dreams about that one special pupil, that one eager and gifted young head into which he can pour all that he knows and loves and who will justify all the years of frustration in the classroom. There have been pupils that I'm proud of, but I've always had to bully them into doing their school work. Not with Thami. *He* wants to learn the way other boys want to run out of the classroom and make mischief. If he looks after himself he'll go far and do big things. He's a born leader, Isabel, and that is what your generation needs. Powerful forces are fighting for the souls of you young people. You need *real* leaders. Not rabblerousers. I know Thami is meant to be one. I know it with such certainty it makes me frightened. Because it is a responsibility. Mine and mine alone.

I've got a small confession to make. In addition to everything I've already said, there's another reason for this idea of mine. When you and Thami shine at the Festival, as I know you will, and win first prize and we've pocketed a nice little cheque for five thousand rand, I am going to point to Thami and say: "And now ladies and gentlemen, a full university scholarship if you please."

ISABEL: And you'll get it. We'll shine, we'll win, we'll pocket that cheque and Thami will get a scholarship.

[MR M'S *turn for an enthusiastic response*]

MR M: Your unruly behaviour is very infectious! [*Embarrassment and laughter*]

ISABEL: *My* unruly behaviour? I like that! I caught that disease in the location, I'll have you know.

MR M: The future is ours, Isabel. We'll show this stupid country how it is done.

ISABEL: When do we start?

MR M: Next week. We need to plan our campaign very carefully.

ISABEL: I'll be ready.

SCENE 4

MR M *alone.*

He talks directly to the audience.

MR M: "I am a man who in the eager pursuit of knowledge forgets his food and in the joy of its attainment forgets his sorrows, and who does not perceive that old age is coming on." [*He shakes his head*] No. As I am sure you have already guessed, that is not me. My pursuit of knowledge is eager, but I do perceive and only too clearly, that old age is coming on, and at the best of times I do a bad job of forgetting my sorrows. Those wonderful words come from the finest teacher I have ever had, that most wise of all the ancient philosophers... Confucius! Yes. I am a Confucian. A black Confucian! There are not many of us. In fact, I think there's a good chance that the only one in the country is talking to you at this moment.

I claim him as my teacher because I have read very carefully, and many times, and I will read it many times more, a little book I have about him, his life, his thoughts and utterances. Truly, they *are* wonderful words my friends, wonderful, wonderful words! My classroom motto comes from its pages: "Learning undigested by thought is labour lost, thought unassisted by learning is perilous!" But the words that challenge me most these days, is something he said towards the end of his life. At the age of seventy he turned to his pupils one day and said that he could do whatever his heart prompted, without transgressing what was right. What do you say to that? Think about it. *Anything* his heart prompted, *anything* that rose up as a spontaneous urge in his soul, *without*

155

transgressing what was right!

What a heart, my friends! Aren't you envious of old Confucius? Wouldn't it be marvellous to have a heart you could trust like that? Imagine being able to wake up in the morning in your little room, yawn and stretch, scratch a few fleabites and then jump out of bed and eat your bowl of mealiepap and sour milk with a happy heart because you know that when you walk out into the world you will be free to obey and act out, with a clear conscience, all the promptings of your heart. No matter what you see out there on that battleground of location streets, and believe me, there are days now when my eyesight feels more like a curse than a blessing, no matter what stories of hardship and suffering you hear, or how bad the news you read in the newspaper, knowing that the whole truth, which can't be printed, is even worse... in spite of all that, you need have no fear of your spontaneous urges, because in obeying them you will not transgress what is right.[*Another shake of his head, another rueful smile*]

No yet again. Not in this life, and most certainly not in this world where I find myself, will those wonderful words of Confucius ever be mine. Not even if I lived to be one hundred and seventy, will I end up with a calm, gentle Chinese heart like his.

I wish I could. Believe me, I really wish I could. Because I am frightened of the one I've got. I don't get gentle promptings from it, my friends. I get heart attacks. When I walk out into those streets, and I see what is happening to my people, it jumps out and savages me like a wild beast. [*Thumping his chest with a clenched fist*] I've got a whole zoo in here, a mad zoo of hungry animals... and the keeper is frightened! All of them. Mad and savage! Look at me! I'm sweating today. I've been sweating for a week. Why? Because one of those animals, the one called Hope, has broken loose and is looking for food. Don't be fooled by its gentle name. It is as dangerous as Hate and Despair would be if they ever managed to break out. You think I'm exaggerating? Pushing my metaphor a little too far? Then I'd like to put you inside a black skin and ask

you to keep Hope alive, find food for it on these streets
where our children, our loved and precious children, go
hungry and die of malnutrition. No, believe me, it is a
dangerous animal for a black man to have prowling
around in his heart. So how do I manage to keep mine
alive, you ask. Friends, I am going to let you into a
terrible secret. That is why I am a teacher.

It is all part of a secret plan to keep alive this savage Hope
of mine. The truth is that I am worse than Nero feeding
Christians to the lions. I feed young people to my Hope.
Every young body behind a school desk keeps it alive.
So you've been warned! If you see a hungry gleam in my
eyes when I look at your children... you know what it
means. That is the monster that stands here before you.
Full name: Anela Myalatya. Age: fifty-seven. Marital
status: bachelor. Occupation: teacher. Address: the back
room of the Reverend Mbopa's house next to the Anglican
Church of Saint Mark. It's a little on the small side. You
know those big kitchen-size boxes of matches they sell
these days... well, if you imagine one of those as Number
One Classroom at Zolile High, then the little matchbox
you put in your pocket is my room at the Reverend
Mbopa's. But I'm not complaining. It has got all I need...
a table and chair where I correct homework and prepare
lessons, a comfortable bed for a good night's insomnia,
and a reserved space for my chair in front of the television
set in the Reverend Mbopa's lounge.

So there you have it. What I call my life rattles around in
these two matchboxes... the classroom and the backroom.
If you see me hurrying along the streets you can be
reasonably certain that one of those two is my urgent
destination. The people tease me. "Faster Mr M" they
shout to me from their front door. "You'll be late." They
think it's a funny joke. They don't know how close they
are to a terrible truth...

Yes! The clocks are ticking, my friends. History has got a
strict timetable. If we're not careful we might be
remembered as the country where everybody arrived too
late.

157

MR M *waiting.*

ISABEL *hurries on, carrying hockey stick, togs and her school
case. She is hot and exhausted.*

ISABEL: Sorry Mr M, sorry. The game started late.

MR M: I haven't been waiting long. [ISABEL *unburdens herself and
collapses with a groan*] Did you win?

ISABEL: No. We played a team of friendly Afrikaans-speaking
young Amazons from Jansenville and they licked us
hollow. Four-one! God they were fit. And fast. They ran
circles around us on that hockey field. I felt so stupid. I
kept saying to myself, "It's only a game, Isabel. Relax!
Enjoy it! Have a good time!" But no, there I was swearing
under my breath at poor little Hilary Castle for being slow
and not getting into position for my passes. [*Laughing at
herself*] You want to know something really terrible? A
couple of times I actually wanted to go over and hit her
with my hockey stick. Isn't that awful? It's no good, Mr
M, I've got to face it: I'm a bad loser. Got any advice for
me?

MR M: On how to be a good one?

ISABEL: Ja. How to lose graciously. With dignity. I mean it.
I really wish I could.

MR M: If I did have advice for you, Isabel, I think I would be well
advised to try it out on myself first...

ISABEL: Why? You one as well? [MR M *nods*] I don't believe it.

MR M: It's true, Isabel. I'm ashamed to say it but when I lose I also
want to grab my hockey stick and hit somebody. [*A good
laugh from* ISABEL] Believe me I can get very petty and
mean if I'm not on the winning side. I suppose most
bachelors end up like that. We get so used to have
everything our own way that when something goes
wrong...!

So there's my advice to you. Get married! If what I've
heard is true holy matrimony is the best school of all for
learning how to lose.

ISABEL: I don't think it's something you can learn. You've either
got it or you haven't. Like Thami. Without even thinking

about it I know *he's* a good loser.

MR M: Maybe.

ISABEL: No. No maybes about it. He'd never grab his hockey stick and take it out on somebody else if he doesn't win.

MR M: You're right. I can't see him doing that. You've become good friends, haven't you?

ISABEL: The best. These past few weeks have been quite an education. I owe you a lot, you know. I think Thami would say the same... if you would only give him the chance to do so.

MR M: What do you mean by that remark, young lady?

ISABEL: You know what I mean by that remark, Mr Teacher! It's called Freedom of Speech.

MR M: I've given him plenty of Freedom, within reasonable limits, but he never uses it.

ISABEL: Because you're *always* the teacher and he's *always* the pupil. Stop teaching him all the time, Mr M. Try just talking to him for a change... you know, like a friend. I bet you in some ways I already know more about Thami than you.

MR M: I dare say that is true. In which case tell me, is he happy?

ISABEL: What do you mean? Happy with what? Us? The competition?

MR M: Yes, and also his schoolwork and... everything else.

ISABEL: Why don't you ask him?

MR M: Because all I'll get is another polite "Yes, Teacher". I thought maybe he had said something to you about the way he really felt.

ISABEL: [*Shaking her head*] The two of you! It's crazy! But ja, he's happy. At least I think he is. He's not a blabber-mouth like me, Mr M. He doesn't give much away... even when we talk about ourselves. I don't know what it was like in your time, but being eighteen years old today is a pretty complicated business as far as we're concerned. If you asked me if I was happy, I'd say Yes, but that doesn't mean I haven't got any problems. I've got plenty and I'm sure it's the same with Thami.

MR M: Thami has told you he's got problems?

ISABEL: Come on, Mr M! We've all got problems. I've got

159

problems, you've got problems, Thami's got problems.

MR M: But did he say what they were?

ISABEL: You're fishing for something, Mr M. What is it?

MR M: Trouble, Isabel. I'm sorry to say it, but I'm fishing for trouble and I'm trying to catch it before it gets too big.

ISABEL: Thami is in trouble?

MR M: Not yet, but he will be if he's not careful. And all his friends as well. It's swimming around everywhere, Isabel. In the classroom, out on the streets.

ISABEL: Oh, you mean that sort of trouble. Is it really as bad as people are saying?

MR M: There's a dangerous, reckless mood in the location. Specially among the young people. Very silly things are being said, Isabel and I've got a suspicion that even sillier things are being whispered among themselves. I know Thami trusts you. I was wondering if he had told you what they were whispering about.

ISABEL: [*Shocked by what* MR M *was asking of her*] Wow! That's a hard one you're asking for, Mr M. Just suppose he had, do you think it would be right for me to tell you. *We* call that splitting, you know, and you're not very popular if you're caught doing it.

MR M: It would be for his own good, Isabel.

ISABEL: Well he hasn't . . . thank God! So I don't have to deal with that one. [*Pause*] If I ever did that to him, and he found out, that would be the end of our friendship you know. I wish you hadn't asked me.

MR M: [*Realising his mistake*] Forgive me Isabel. I'm just over-anxious on his behalf. One silly mistake now could ruin everything. Forget that I asked you and . . . please . . . don't mention anything about our little chat to Thami. I'll find time to have a word with him myself.

[THAMI *appears. Also direct from the sports field.*]

THAMI: Hi folks. Sorry I'm late.

ISABEL: I've just got here myself. Mr M is the one who's been waiting.

THAMI: Sorry, teacher. The game went into extra time.

ISABEL: Did you win.

THAMI: No. We lost one-nil.

ISABEL: Good.

THAMI: But it was a good game. We're trying out some new combinations and they nearly worked. The chaps are really starting to come together as a team. A little more practice, that's all we need.

ISABEL: Hear that, Mr M? What did I tell you? And look at him. Smiling! Happy! Even in defeat, a generous word for his team-mates.

THAMI: What's going on?

ISABEL: Don't try to look innocent, Mbikwana. Your secret is out. Your true identity has been revealed. You are a good loser, and don't try to deny it.

THAMI: Me? You're wrong. I don't like losing.

ISABEL: It's not a question of liking or not liking, but of being able to do so without a crooked smile on your face, a knot in your stomach and murder in your heart.

THAMI: You lost your game this afternoon.

ISABEL: Whatever made you guess! We were trounced. So be careful. I'm looking for revenge.

MR M: Good! Then lets see if you can get it in the arena of English literature. What do we deal with today?

THAMI: Nineteenth-century poetry.

MR M: [*With relish*] Beautiful! Beautiful! Beautiful! [*Making himself comfortable*] Whose service?
[THAMI *picks up a stone, hands behind his back, then clenched fists for* ISABEL *to guess. She does. She wins. Their relationship is now obviously very relaxed and easy.*]

ISABEL: Gird your loins, Mbikwana. I want blood.

THAMI: I wish you the very best of luck.

ISABEL: God, I hate you.

MR M: First service, please.

ISABEL: Right. I'll give you an easy one to start with. The Lake Poets. Name them.

THAMI: Wordsworth...

ISABEL: Yes, he was one. Who else?

THAMI: Wordsworth and...

ISABEL: There was only one Wordsworth.

THAMI: I pass.

ISABEL: Wordsworth, Southey and Coleridge.

THAMI: I should have guessed, Coleridge!

MR M: One-love.

ISABEL: First line of a poem by each of them, please.

THAMI: Query, Mr Umpire... how many questions is that?

MR M: One at a time please, Isabel.

ISABEL: Coleridge.

THAMI: "In Xanadu did Kubla Khan
    A stately pleasure dome decree"... And if you don't like
    that one, what about:
    "Tis the middle of the night by the castle clock
    And the owls have awakened the crowing cock
    Tu-whit Tu-whoo."
    And if you're still not satisfied...

ISABEL: Stop showing off, young man.

MR M: One-all.

ISABEL: Wordsworth.

THAMI: "Earth has not anything to show more fair:
    Dull would he be of soul who could pass by
    A sight so touching in its majesty"...

MR M: One-two.

ISABEL: Southey.

THAMI: Pass.

ISABEL: "From his brimstone bed, at break of day
    A-walking the devil is gone,...
    His coat was red and his breeches were blue,
    And there was a hole where his tail came through."

THAMI: Hey, I like that one!

ISABEL: A Poet Laureate to boot.

MR M: Two-all.

ISABEL: One of them was expelled from school. Who was it and
    why?

THAMI: Wordsworth. For smoking in the lavatory.

ISABEL: [*After a good laugh*] You're terrible, Thami. He should
    be penalised, Mr Umpire... for irreverence! It was
    Southey and the reason he was expelled — you're going to
    like this — was for writing a 'precocious' essay about
    flogging.

THAMI: How about that!

MR M: Three-two. Change service.

162

THAMI: I am not going to show you any mercy. What poet was
 born with deformed feet, accused of incest and died of
 fever while helping the Greeks fight for freedom? "A love
 of liberty characterises his poems and the desire to see the
 fettered nations of Europe set free."

ISABEL: Byron.

THAMI: Lord Byron, if you please.

MR M: Two-four.

ISABEL: One of your favourites.

THAMI: You bet.

 "Yet, Freedom! yet thy banner, torn, but flying,
 Streams like the thunder-storm *against* the wind."

 Do you know the Christian names of Lord Byron?

ISABEL: Oh dammit!... it's on the tip of my tongue. Henry?
 [THAMI *shakes his head*] Herbert?

THAMI: How many guesses does she get, Mr Umpire.

ISABEL: All right, give him the point. I pass.

THAMI: George Gordon.

MR M: Three-four.

THAMI: To who was he unhappily married for one long year?

ISABEL: Pass.

THAMI: Anne Isabella Milbanke.

MR M: Four-all.

THAMI: Father's occupation?

ISABEL: Pass.

THAMI: John Byron was a captain in the army.

MR M: Five-four.

THAMI: What other great poet was so overcome with grief when
 he heard news of Byron's death, that he went out and
 carved into a rock: "Byron is dead."

ISABEL: Matthew Arnold?

THAMI: No. Another aristocrat... Alfred, Lord Tennyson.

MR M: Six-four. Change service.

ISABEL: Right. Whose body did your Lord Byron burn on a beach
 in Italy?

THAMI: Shelley.

MR M: Four-seven.

ISABEL: And what happened to Mr Shelley's ashes?

THAMI: In a grave beside John Keats in Rome.

163

MR M: Four-eight.

ISABEL: Shelley's wife. What is she famous for?

THAMI: Which one? There were two. Harriet Westbrook, sixteen years old, who he abandoned after three years and who drowned herself? Or number two wife — who I think is the one you're interested in — Mary Wollstonecraft, the author of *Frankenstein*?

MR M: Four-nine.

ISABEL: How much?

MR M: Four-nine.

ISABEL: I don't believe this! [*She grabs her hockey stick*]

THAMI: [*Enjoying himself immensely*] I crammed in two poets last night, Isabel. Guess who they were?

ISABEL: Byron and Shelley. In that case we will deal with Mr John Keats. What profession did he abandon in order to devote himself to poetry.

THAMI: Law.

ISABEL: You're guessing and you're wrong. He qualified as a surgeon.

MR M: Five-nine.

ISABEL: What epitaph, composed by himself, is engraved on his tombstone in Rome?

THAMI: Pass.

ISABEL: "Here lies one whose name was writ on water."

MR M: Six-nine. Let's leave the Births, Marriages and Deaths column, please. I want to hear some more poetry.

THAMI: Whose service?

MR M: Yours.

THAMI: "I must go down to the seas again, to the lonely sea and the sky,
And all I ask is a tall ship and a star to steer her by..."

ISABEL: "And the wheel's kick and the wind's song and the white sail's shaking,
And a grey mist on the sea's face and a grey dawn breaking.
I must go down to the seas again, to the vagrant gypsy life,
To the gull's way and the whale's way where the wind's like a whetted knife..."

THAMI: "And all I ask is a merry yarn from a laughing fellow-rover,

And a quiet sleep and a sweet dream when the long trek's
over."

MR M: Bravo! Bravo! Bravo! But who gets the point?

ISABEL: Give it to John Masefield, Mr Umpire. [*To* THAMI]
Nineteenth century?

THAMI: He was born in 1878. To tell you the truth I couldn't resist
it. You choose one.

ISABEL: "I met a traveller from an antique land
Who said: Two vast and trunkless legs of stone
Stand in the desert... near them, on the sand,
Half sunk, a shattered visage lies, whose frown
And wrinkled lip, and sneer of cold command,
Tell that its sculptor well those passions read
Which yet survive, stamped on these lifeless things
The hand that mocked them, and the heart that fed:
And on the pedestal these words appear:"

THAMI: "My name is Ozymandias, King of Kings:
Look on my work, ye mighty, and despair!"

ISABEL: "Nothing beside remains. Round the decay
Of that colossal wreck, boundless and bare
The lone and level sands stretch far away."

THAMI: And that point goes to Mr Shelley.

ISABEL: [*Notebook from her school case*] You'll be interested to
know, gentlemen, that Ozymandias is not a fiction of Mr
Shelley's very fertile imagination. He was in fact a real,
live Egyptian king. Rameses the second! According to
Everyman's Encyclopedia, "One of the most famous of
Egyptian kings... erected many monuments... his
oppressive rule left Egypt impoverished and suffering from
an incurable decline."

THAMI: What happened to the statue?

ISABEL: You mean how it was toppled?

THAMI: Yes.

ISABEL: Didn't say. Weather, I suppose. And time. Two thousand
four hundred BC... that's over four thousand years ago.
Why? What were you thinking?

THAMI: I had a book of Bible stories when I was small, and there
was a picture in it showing the building of the pyramids by
the slaves. Thousands of them, like ants, pulling the big

blocks of stone with ropes, being guarded by soldiers with whips and spears. According to that picture the slaves must have easily outnumbered the soldiers one hundred to one. I actually tried to count them all one day but the drawing wasn't good enough for that.

ISABEL: What are you up to, Mbikwana? Trying to stir up a little social unrest in the time of the pharaohs, are you?

THAMI: Don't joke about it, Miss Dyson. There are quite a few Ozymandiases in this country waiting to be toppled. And with any luck you'll live to see it happen. *We* won't leave it to Time to bring them down.

[MR M *has been listening to the exchange between* THAMI *and* ISABEL *very attentively.*]

MR M: [*Trying to put a smile on it*] Who is the *we* you speak for with such authority, Thami?

THAMI: The People.

MR M: [*Recognition*]Yes, yes, yes, of course ... I should have known. The People ... with a capital P. Does that include me? Am I one of The People?

THAMI: If you choose to be.

MR M: I've got to choose, have I? My black skin doesn't confer automatic membership. So how do I go about choosing?

THAMI: By identifying with the fight for our Freedom.

MR M: As simple as that? I want our Freedom as much as any of you. In fact, I was fighting for it in my small way long before any of you were born! But I've got a small problem. Does that noble fight of ours really have to stoop to pulling down a few silly statues? Where do you get the idea that we, The People, want you to do that for us?

THAMI: [*Trying*] They are not our heroes, teacher.

MR M: They are not our statues, Thami! Wouldn't it be better for us to rather put our energies into erecting a few of our own? We've also got heroes, you know.

THAMI: Like who, Mr M? Nelson Mandela? [*Shaking his head with disbelief*] Hey! *They* would pull *that* statue down so fast...

MR M: [*Cutting him*] In which case they would be just as guilty of gross vandalism ... because that is what it will be, regardless of who does it to whom. Destroying somebody

166

else's property is inexcusable behaviour.

No, Thami. As one of the People you claim to be acting for, I raise my hand in protest. Please don't pull down any statues on my behalf. Don't use me as an excuse for an act of lawlessness. If you want to do something 'revolutionary' for me let us sit down and discuss it, because I have a few constructive alternatives I would like to suggest. Do I make myself clear?

THAMI: Yes, teacher.

MR M: Good. I'm glad we understand each other.

ISABEL: [*Intervening*] So, what's next? Mr M? How about singling out a few specific authors who we know will definitely come up? Like Dickens. I bet you anything you like there'll be questions about him and his work.

MR M: Good idea. We'll concentrate on novelists. A short list of hot favourites.

ISABEL: Thomas Hardy... Jane Austen... who else, Thami?

MR M: Put your heads together and make a list. I want twenty names. Divide it between the two of you and get to work... I must be on my way.

ISABEL: Just before you go, Mr M, I've got an invitation for you and Thami from my Mom and Dad. Would the two of you like to come to tea one afternoon?

MR M: What a lovely idea!

ISABEL: They've had enough of me going on and on about the all-knowing Mr M and his brilliant protégé, Thami. They want to meet you for themselves. Thami? All right with you?

MR M: Of course we accept, Isabel. It will be a pleasure and a privilege for us to meet Mr and Mrs Dyson. Tell them we accept most gratefully.

ISABEL: Next Sunday.

MR M: Perfect.

ISABEL: Thami?

MR M: Don't worry about him, Isabel. I'll put it in my diary and remind him at school.

[MR M *leaves.*]

ISABEL: [*Sensitive to a change of mood in Thami*] I think you'll like my folks. My Mom's a bit on the reserved side but that's ·

just because she's basically very shy. But you and my Dad should get on well. Start talking sport with him and he won't let you go. He played cricket for E.P., you know.[*Pause*] You will come, won't you?

THAMI: [*Edge to his voice*] Didn't you hear Mr M? "A delight and privilege! We accept most gratefully." [*Writing in notebook*] Charles Dickens ... Thomas Hardy ... Jane Austen ...

ISABEL: Was he speaking for you as well?

THAMI: He speaks for me on nothing!

ISABEL: Relax. I know that. That's why I tried to ask you separately and why I'll ask you again. Would you like to come to tea next Sunday to meet my family? It's not a polite invitation. They really want to meet you.

THAMI: Me? Why? Are they starting to get nervous?

ISABEL: Oh come off it, Thami. Don't be like that. They're always nervous when it comes to me. But this time it happens to be genuine interest. I've told you. I talk about you at home. They know I have a good time with you ... that we're a team ... which they are now very proud of incidentally ... and that we're cramming like lunatics so that we can put up a good show at the festival. Is it so strange that they want to meet you after all that? Honestly, sometimes dealing with the two of you is like walking on a tight-rope. I'm always scared I'm going to put a foot wrong and ... well, I just *hate* being scared like that. [*A few seconds of truculent silence between the two of them*] What's going on, Thami? Between you two? There's something very wrong, isn't there?

THAMI: No more than usual.

ISABEL: No you don't. A hell of a lot more than usual and don't deny it because it's getting to be pretty obvious. I mean, I know he gets on your nerves. I knew that the first day we met. But it's more than that now. These past couple of meetings I've caught you looking at him, watching him in a ... I don't know ... in a sort of hard way. Very critical. Not just once. Many times. Do you know you're doing it? [*Shrug of the shoulders from* THAMI] Well, if you know it or not, you are. And now he's started as well.

168

THAMI: What do you mean?

ISABEL: He's watching you.

THAMI: So? He can watch me as much as he likes. I've got nothing
to hide. Even if I did he'd be the last person to find out.
He sees nothing, Isabel.

ISABEL: I think you are very wrong.

THAMI: No I'm not. That's his trouble. He's got eyes and ears
but he sees and hears nothing.

ISABEL: Go on. Please. [*Pause*] I mean it, Thami. I want to know
what's going on.

THAMI: He is out of touch with what is really happening to us
blacks and the way we feel about things. He thinks the
world is still the way it was when he was young. It's not!
It's different now, but he's too blind to see it. He doesn't
open his eyes and ears and see what is happening around
him or listen to what the people are saying.

ISABEL: What are they saying?

THAMI: They've got no patience left, Isabel. They want change.
They want it now!

ISABEL: But he agrees with that. He never stops saying it himself.

THAMI: No. His ideas about change are the old-fashioned ones.
And what have they achieved? Nothing. We are worse off
now than we ever were. The people don't want to listen to
his kind of talk any more.

ISABEL: I'm still lost, Thami. What sort of talk is that?

THAMI: You've just heard it, Isabel. It calls our struggle vandalism
and lawless behaviour. It's the sort of talk that expects us
to do nothing and wait quietly for White South Africa to
wake up. If we listen to it our grandchildren still won't
know what it means to be free.

ISABEL: And those old-fashioned ideas of his ... are we one of
them?

THAMI: What do you mean?

ISABEL: You and me. The competition.

THAMI: Let's change the subject, Isabel. [*His notebook*] Charles
Dickens ... Thomas Hardy ... Jane Austen ...

ISABEL: No! You can't do that! I'm involved. I've got a right to
know. Are we an old-fashioned idea?

THAMI: Not our friendship. That is our decision, our choice.

169

ISABEL: And the competition?

THAMI: [*Uncertain of himself*] Maybe ... I'm not sure. I need time to think about it.

ISABEL: [*Foreboding*] Oh boy. This doesn't sound so good. You've got to talk to him, Thami.

THAMI: He won't listen.

ISABEL: Make him listen!

THAMI: It doesn't work that way with us, Isabel. You can't just stand up and tell your teacher he's got the wrong ideas.

ISABEL: Well, that's just your bad luck because you are going to have to do it. Even if it means breaking sacred rules and traditions, you have got to stand up and have it out with him. I don't think you realise what all of this means to him. It's a hell of a lot more than just an old-fashioned idea as far as he's concerned. This competition, you and me, but especially you, Thami Mbikwana, have become a sort of crowning achievement to his life as a teacher. It's become a sort of symbol for him, and if it were to all suddenly collapse...! No. I don't want to think about it.

THAMI: [*Flash of anger and impatience*] Then don't! Please leave it alone now and just let's get on with whatever it is we've got to do.

ISABEL: Right, if that's the way you want it ... [*Her notebook*] Charles Dickens, Thomas Hardy, Jane Austen ... who else?

THAMI: I'm sorry. I know you're only trying to help but you've got to understand that it's not just a personal issue between him and me. That would be easy. I don't even think I would care then. Just wait for the end of the year and then get out of that classroom and that school as fast as I can. But there is more to it than that. I've told you before: sitting in a classroom doesn't mean the same thing to me that it does to you. That classroom is a political reality in my life ... it's part of the whole political system we're up against and Mr M has chosen to identify himself with it.

ISABEL: [*Trying a new tack*] All right. I believe you. I accept everything you said ... about him, your relationship, the situation ... no arguments. Okay? But doesn't all of that only make it still more important that the two of you start

170

talking to each other? I know *he* wants to, but he doesn't know how to start. It's *so* sad ... because I can see him trying to reach out to you. Show him how it's done. Make the first move. Oh Thami, don't let it go wrong between the two of you. That's just about the worst thing I could imagine. We all need each other.

THAMI: I don't need him.

ISABEL: I think you do, just as much as he ...

THAMI: Don't tell me what I need, Isabel! And stop telling me what to do! You don't know what my life is about, so keep your advice to yourself.

ISABEL: I'm sorry. I didn't mean to interfere. I thought we were a team and that what involved you two concerned me as well. I'll mind my own business in future. [*She is deeply hurt. She collects her things*] Let's leave it at that then. See you next week ... I hope!

[*Starts to leave, stops, returns and confronts him*] You used the word 'friendship' a few minutes ago. It's a beautiful word and I'll do anything to make it true for us. But don't let's cheat, Thami. If we can't be open and honest with each other and say what is in our hearts, we've got no right to use it.

[*She leaves.*]

SCENE 6

THAMI *alone.*

THAMI: [*Singing*]
Masiye Masiye Skolweni
Masiye Masiye Skolweni
eskolweni Sasakhaya
eskolweni Sasakhaya [*Repeat*]

Gonqo Gonqo
Iyakhala Intsimbi
Gonqo Gonqo
Iyakhala Intsimbi

[*Translating*]
Come, come, let's go to school

171

Let's go to our very own school
Gonqo Gonqo
The bell is ringing
Gonqo Gonqo
The bell is calling!

Singing that at the top of his voice and holding his slate under his arm, seven-year-old Thami Mbikwana marched proudly with the other children every morning into his classroom.

Gonqo Gonqo
The school bell is ringing!

And what a wonderful sound that was for me.

Starting with that little farm school, I remember my school bells like beautiful voices calling to me all through my childhood... and I came running when they did. You should have seen me, man. In junior school I was the first one at the gates every morning. I was waiting there when the caretaker came to unlock them. Oh yes! Young Thami was a very eager scholar. And what made it even better, he was also one of the clever ones. A 'most particularly promising pupil' is how one of my school reports described me. My first real scholastic achievement was a composition I wrote about myself in Standard Two. Not only did it get me top marks in the class, the teacher was so proud of me, she made me read it out to the whole school at assembly.

[*His composition*] "The story of my life so far. By Thami Mbikwana.

The story of my life so far is not yet finished because I am only ten years old and I am going to live a long, long time.

I come from King William's Town. My father is Amos Mbikwana and he works very hard for the baas on the railway. I am also going to work very hard and get good marks in all my classes and make my teacher very happy. The story of my life so far has also got a very happy ending because when I am big I am going to be a doctor so that I can help my people. I will drive to the hospital every day in a big, white ambulance full of nurses. I will

172

make black people better free of charge. The white people must pay for my medicine because they have got lots of money. That way I will also get lots of money. My mother and my father will stop working and come and live with me in a big house. That is the story of my life up to where I am now in Standard Two."

I must bring my story up to date because there have been some changes and developments since little Thami wrote those hopeful words eight years ago. To start with I don't think I want to be a doctor any more. That praiseworthy ambition has unfortunately died in me. It still upsets me very much when I think about the pain and suffering of my people, but I realise now that what causes most of it is not an illness that can be cured by the pills and bottles of medicine they hand out at the clinic. I don't need to go to university to learn what my people really want is a strong double-dose of that traditional old Xhosa remedy called 'Inkululeko. Freedom.' So right now I'm not sure what I want to be any more. It's hard, you see, for us 'bright young blacks' to dream about wonderful careers as doctors, or lawyers when we keep waking up in a world which doesn't allow the majority of our people any dreams at all. But to get back to my composition, I did try my best to keep that promise I made in it. For a long time... Standard Three, Standard Four, Standard Five... I did work very hard and I did get good marks in all my subjects. This 'most particularly promising pupil' made a lot of teachers very happy.

I'm sorry to say but I can't do it any more. I have tried very hard, believe me, but it is not as simple and easy as it used to be to sit behind that desk and listen to the teacher. That little world of the classroom where I used to be happy, where they used to pat me on the head and say: Little Thami, you'll go far... that little room of wonderful promises, where I used to feel so safe has become a place I don't trust any more. Now I sit at my desk like an animal that has smelt danger, heard something moving in the bushes and knows it must be very, very careful.

At the beginning of this year the Inspector of Bantu

Schools in the Cape Midlands Region, Mr Dawid
Grobbelaar — he makes us call him Oom Dawie — came
to give us Standard Tens his usual pep-talk. He does it
every year. We know Oom Dawie well. He's been coming
to Zolile for a long time. When he walked into our
classroom we all jumped up as usual but he didn't want
any of that. "Sit, sit! I'm not a bloody sergeant major."
Oom Dawie believes he knows how to talk to us. He
loosened his tie, took off his jacket and rolled up his
sleeves. It was a very hot day.

"Dis beter. Nou kan ons lekker gesels. Boys and girls or
maybe I should say young men and young women now,
because you are coming to the end of your time behind
those desks... you are special! You are the elite! We have
educated you because we want you to be major
shareholders in the future of this wonderful Republic of
ours. In fact, we want *all* the peoples of South Africa to
share in that future... black, white, brown, yellow, and if
there are some green ones out there, then them as well.
Ho! Ho! Ho!"

I don't remember much about what he said after that
because my head was trying to deal with that one word:
the future! He kept using it... "our future" "the country's
future", "a wonderful future of peace and prosperity."
What does he really mean, I kept asking myself? Why does
my heart go hard and tight as a stone when he says it? I
look around me in the location at the men and women
who went out into that wonderful future before me. What
do I see? Happy and contented shareholders in this
exciting enterprise called the Republic of South Africa?
No. I see a generation of tired, defeated men and women
crawling back to their miserable little pondoks at the end
of a day's work for the white baas or madam. And those
are the lucky ones. They've at least got work. Most of
them are just sitting around wasting away their lives while
they wait helplessly for a miracle to feed their families, a
miracle that never comes.

Those men and women are our fathers and mothers. We
have grown up watching their humiliation. We have to live

174

every day with the sight of them begging for food in this land of their birth, and their parents' birth . . . all the way back to the first proud ancestors of our people. Black people lived on this land for centuries before any white settler had landed! Does Oom Dawie think we are blind? That when we walk through the streets of the white town we do not see the big houses and beautiful gardens with their swimming pools full of laughing people, and compare it with what we've got, what we have to call home? Or does Oom Dawie just think we are very stupid? That in spite of the wonderful education he has given us, we can't use the simple arithmetic of add and subtract, multiply and divide to work out the rightful share of twenty-five million black people?

Do you understand me, good people? Do you understand now why it is not as easy as it used to be to sit behind that desk and learn only what Oom Dawie has decided I must know? My head is rebellious. It refuses now to remember when the Dutch landed, and the Huguenots landed, and the British landed. It has already forgotten when the old Union became the proud young Republic. But it does know what happened in Kliptown in 1955, in Sharpeville on 21st March, 1960, and in Soweto on the 16th of June, 1976. Do you? Better find out because those are dates your children will have to learn one day. We don't need the Zolile classrooms any more. We know now what they really are . . . traps which have been carefully set to catch our minds, our souls. No, good people. We have woken up at last. We have found another school . . . the streets, the little rooms, the funeral parlours of the location . . . anywhere the people meet and whisper names we have been told to forget, the dates of events they try to tell us never happened, and the speeches they try to say were never made. Those are the lessons we are eager and proud to learn, because they are lessons about *our* history, about *our* heroes. But the time for whispering them is past. Tomorrow we start shouting.

AMANDLA!

ACT TWO

SCENE 1

ISABEL *and* THAMI. *She has books and papers. Behind a relaxed and easy manner, she watches* THAMI *carefully.*

ISABEL: What I've done is write out a sort of condensed biography of all of them... you know, the usual stuff... date of birth, where they were born, where they died, who they married... et cetera, et cetera. My Dad made copies for you and Mr M. Sit. [*Hands over a set of papers to* THAMI] You okay?

THAMI: Ja, ja.

ISABEL: For example... [*Reading*] Brontë sisters... I lumped them all together... Charlotte 1816 to 1855; Emily 1818 to 1848; Anne 1820 to 1849... Can you believe that? Not one of them reached the age of forty. Anne died when she was twenty-nine, Emily when she was thirty, and Charlotte reached the ripe old age of thirty-nine! Family home: Haworth, Yorkshire. First publication a joint volume of verse, *Poems by Currer, Ellis and Acton Bell*. All novels published under these *nom-de-plumes*. Charlotte the most prolific... [*Abandoning the notes*] Why am I doing this? You're not listening to me.

THAMI: Sorry.

ISABEL: [*She waits for more, but that is all she gets*] So? Should I carry on wasting my breath or do you want to say something?

THAMI: No, I must talk.

ISABEL: Good. I'm ready to listen.

THAMI: I don't know where to begin.

ISABEL: The deep end. Take my advice, go to the deep end and just jump right in. That's how I learnt to swim.

THAMI: No. I want to speak carefully because I don't want you to get the wrong ideas about what's happening and what I'm going to say. It's not like it's your fault, that it's because of anything you said or did... you know what I mean?

ISABEL: You don't want me to take personally whatever it is you are finding so hard to tell me.

176

THAMI: That's right. It's not about you and me personally. I've had a good time with you, Isabel.

ISABEL: I've had an important one with you.

THAMI: If it was just you and me, there wouldn't be a problem.

ISABEL: We've got a problem, have we?

THAMI: I have.

ISABEL: [*Losing patience*] Oh for God's sake, Thami. Stop trying to spare my feelings and just say it! If you are trying to tell me that I've been wasting my breath for a lot longer than just this afternoon... just go ahead and say it! I'm not a child. I can take it. Because that is what you are trying to tell me, isn't it? That it's all off.

THAMI: Yes.

ISABEL: The great literary quiz team is no more. You are pulling out of the competition.

THAMI: Yes.

ISABEL: You shouldn't have made it so hard for yourself, Thami. It doesn't come as all that big a surprise. I've had a feeling that something was going to go wrong somewhere.

Been a strange time these past few weeks, hasn't it? At home, at school, in the shop... everywhere! Things I've been seeing and doing my whole life, just don't feel right any more. Like my Saturday chats with Samuel — I told you about him, remember, he delivers for my Dad — well you should have heard the last one. It was excruciating. It felt so false, and forced, and when I listened to what I was saying and how I was saying it... oh my God! Sounded as if I thought I was talking to a ten-year-old. Halfway through our misery my Dad barged in and told me not to waste Samuel's time because he had work to do which of course led to a flaming row between me and my Dad. Am I changing, Thami? My Dad says I am.

THAMI: In what way?

ISABEL: Forget it. The only thing I *do* know at this moment is that I don't very much like the way anything feels right now, starting with myself. So have you told Mr M yet?

THAMI: No.

ISABEL: Good luck. I don't envy you that little conversation. If I'm finding the news a bit hard to digest, I don't know

177

what he is going to do with it. I've just got to accept it. I
doubt very much if he will.

THAMI: He's got no choice, Isabel. I've decided and that's the end
of it.

ISABEL: So do you think we can at least talk about it? Help me to
understand? Because to be absolutely honest with you,
Thami, I don't think I do. You're not the only one with a
problem. I've also got a big one. What Mr M had to say
about the team and the whole idea made a hell of a lot of
sense to me.

You owe it to me, Thami. A lot more than just my spare
time is involved.

THAMI: Talk about what? Don't you know what is going on?

ISABEL: Don't be stupid, Thami! Of course I do! You'd have to be
pretty dumb not to know that the dreaded 'unrest' has
finally reached us as well.

THAMI: We don't call it that. Our word for it is Isiqalo...
The Beginning.

ISABEL: All right then, The Beginning. I don't care what it's
called. All I'm asking you to do is explain to me how the
two of us learning some poetry, cramming in potted
bios... interferes with all of that.

THAMI: Please just calm down and listen to me! I know you're
angry and I don't blame you. I would be as well. But you
must understand that pulling out of this competition is just
a small side issue. There was a meeting in the location last
night. It was decided to call for a general stay-at-home.
We start boycotting classes tomorrow as part of that
campaign.

ISABEL: Does Mr M know about all of this?

THAMI: I think he does now.

ISABEL: Wasn't he at the meeting?

THAMI: The meeting was organised by the Comrades. He wasn't
welcome.

ISABEL: Because his ideas are old-fashioned.

THAMI: Yes.

ISABEL: School boycott! Comrades! So our safe, contented little
Camdeboo is really going to find out what it's all about.
How long do you think it will last?

178

THAMI: I don't know. It's hard to say.

ISABEL: A week?

THAMI: No. It will be longer.

ISABEL: A month? Two months?

THAMI: We'll go back to school when the authorities scrap Bantu Education and recognise and negotiate with Student Committees. That was the resolution last night.

ISABEL: But when the boycott and... you know... everything is all over could we carry on then, if there was still time?

THAMI: I haven't thought about that.

ISABEL: So think about it. Please.

THAMI: [*Nervous about a commitment*] It's hard to say, Isabel... but ja... maybe we could... I'm not sure.

ISABEL: Not much enthusiasm there, Mr Mbikwana! You're right. Why worry about a stupid competition? It will most probably be too late anyway. So that's it then. Let's just say we gave ourselves a crash course in English literature. Could have done a lot worse with our spare time, couldn't we? I enjoyed myself. I read a lot of beautiful poetry I might never have got around to. [*Uncertain of herself*] It doesn't mean the end of everything though, does it? I mean... can we go on meeting, just as friends?

THAMI: [*Warily*] When?

ISABEL: Oh... I mean, you know, like any time. Next week! [*Pause*] I'm not talking about the competition, Thami. I accept that it's dead. I think it's a pity... but so what. I'm talking now about you and me, just as friends.
[*She waits. She realises. She collects herself*] So our friendship *is* an old-fashioned idea after all. Well don't waste your time here. You better get going and look after... whatever it is that's beginning. And good luck! [THAMI *starts to go*] No! Thami come back here!!
[*Struggling ineffectually to control her anger and pain*] There is something very stupid somewhere and it's most probably me but I can't help it... *it just doesn't make sense!* I know it does to you and I'm sure it's just my white selfishness and ignorance that is stopping me from understanding, *but it still doesn't make sense.* Why can't we go on seeing each other and meeting as friends? Tell me

179

what is wrong with our friendship?

THAMI: You're putting words in my mouth, Isabel. I didn't say there was anything wrong with it. But others won't see it the way we do.

ISABEL: Who? Your Comrades?

THAMI: Yes.

ISABEL: And they are going to decide whether we can or can't be friends!

THAMI: I was right. You don't understand what's going on.

ISABEL: And you're certainly not helping me to.

THAMI: [*Trying*] Visiting you like this is dangerous. People talk. Your maid has seen me. She could mention, just innocently but to the wrong person, that Thami Mbikwana is visiting and having tea with the white people she works for.

ISABEL: And of course that is such a big crime!

THAMI: In the eyes of the location... yes! My world is also changing, Isabel. I'm breaking the boycott by being here. The Comrades don't want any mixing with whites. They have ordered that contact must be kept at a minimum.

ISABEL: And you go along with that?

THAMI: Yes.

ISABEL: Happily!

THAMI: [*Goaded by her lack of understanding*] Yes! I go along happily with that!!

ISABEL: Hell Thami, this great Beginning of yours sounds like ... [*Shakes her head*]... I don't know. Other people deciding who can and who can't be your friends, what you must do and what you can't do. Is this the Freedom you've been talking to me about? That you were going to fight for?

[MR M *enters quietly. His stillness is a disturbing contrast to the bustle and energy we have come to associate with him.*]

MR M: Don't let me interrupt you. Please carry on.
[*To* THAMI] I'm most interested in your reply to that question. [*Pause*] I think he's forgotten what it was, Isabel. Ask him again.

ISABEL: [*Backing out of the confrontation*] No. Forget it.

MR M: [*Persisting*] Isabel was asking you how you managed to

180

reconcile your desire for Freedom with what the Comrades are doing.

ISABEL: I said forget it, Mr M. I'm not interested any more.

MR M: [*Insistent*] But I am.

THAMI: The Comrades are imposing a discipline which our struggle needs at this point. There is no comparison between that and the total denial of our Freedom by the white government. They have been forcing on us an inferior education in order to keep us permanently suppressed. When our struggle is successful there will be no more need for the discipline the Comrades are demanding.

MR M: [*Grudging admiration*] Oh Thami . . . you learn your lessons so well! The 'revolution' has only just begun and you are already word perfect. So then tell me, do you think I agree with this inferior Bantu Education that is being forced on you?

THAMI: You teach it.

MR M: But unhappily so! Most unhappily, unhappily so! Don't you know that? Did you have your fingers in your ears the thousand times I've said so in the classroom? Where were you when I stood there and said that I regarded it as my duty, my deepest obligation to you young men and women to sabotage it, and that my conscience would not let me rest until I had succeeded. And I have! Yes, I have succeeded! I have got irrefutable proof of my success. You! Yes. You can stand here and accuse me, unjustly, because I have also had a struggle and I have won mine. I have liberated your mind in spite of what the Bantu Education was trying to do to it. Your mouthful of big words and long sentences which the not-so-clever comrades are asking you to speak and write for them, your wonderful eloquence at last night's meeting which got them all so excited — yes, I heard about it! — you must thank me for all of that, Thami.

THAMI: No I don't. You never taught me those lessons.

MR M: Oh I see. You have got other teachers, have you?

THAMI: Yes. Yours were lessons in whispering. There are men now who are teaching us to shout. Those little tricks and

181

jokes of yours in the classroom liberated nothing. The struggle doesn't need the big English words you taught me how to spell.

MR M: Be careful, Thami. Be careful! Be careful! Don't scorn words. They are sacred! Magical! Yes, they are. Do you know that without words a man can't think? Yes, it's true. Take that thought back with you as a present from the despised Mr M and share it among the Comrades. Tell them the difference between a man and an animal is that Man thinks, and he thinks with words. Consider the mighty ox. Four powerful legs, massive shoulders, and a beautiful thick hide that gave our warriors shields to protect them when they went into battle. Think of his beautiful head Thami, the long horns, the terrible bellow from his lungs when he charges a rival! *But it has got no words and therefore it is stupid!* And along comes that funny little, hairless animal that has got only two thin legs, no horns and a skin worth nothing and he tells that ox what to do. He is its master and he is that because he can speak! If the struggle needs weapons give it words, Thami. Stones and petrol bombs can't get inside those armoured cars. Words can. They can do something even more devastating than that . . . they can get inside the heads of those inside the armoured cars. I speak to you like this because if I have faith in anything, it is faith in the power of the word. Like my master, the great Confucius, I believe that, using only words, a man can right a wrong and judge and execute the wrongdoer. You are meant to use words like that.

Talk to others. Bring them back into the classroom. They will listen to you. They look up to you as a leader.

THAMI: No, I won't. You talk about them as if they were a lot of sheep waiting to be led. They know what they are doing. They'd call me a traitor if I tried to persuade them otherwise.

MR M: Then listen carefully, Thami. I have received instructions from the department to make a list of all those who take part in the boycott. Do you know what they will do with that list when all this is over . . . because don't fool yourself, Thami, it will be. When your boycott comes to an inglorious end like all the others ... they will make all of you apply for re-admission and if your name is on that list ... [*He leaves the rest unspoken*]

THAMI: Will you do it? Will you make that list for them?

MR M: That is none of your business.

THAMI: Then don't ask me questions about mine.

MR M: [*His control finally snaps. He explodes with anger and bitterness*] Yes, I will! I will ask you all the questions I like. And you know why? Because I am a man and you are a boy. And if you are not in that classroom tomorrow you will be a very, very silly boy.

THAMI: Then don't call me names, Mr M.

MR M: No? Then what must I call you? Comrade Thami? Never! You are a silly boy now, and without an education you will grow up to be a stupid man!
[*For a moment it looks as if* THAMI *is going to leave without saying anything more, but he changes his mind and confronts* MR M *for the last time.*]

THAMI: The others called *you* names at the meeting last night. Did your spies tell you that? Government stooge, sell-out collaborator. They said you licked the white man's arse and would even eat his shit if it meant keeping your job. Did your spies tell you that I tried to stop them saying those things?
Don't wait until tomorrow to make your list, Mr M. You can start now. Write down the first name: Thami Mbikwana.
[*He leaves*]
[*A few seconds of silence after* THAMI'S *departure.* ISABEL *makes a move towards* MR M *but he raises his hand sharply, stopping her, keeping her at a distance.*]

ISABEL: This fucking country!
[*She leaves.*]

SCENE 2

MR M *alone.*
To start with his mood is one of quiet, vacant disbelief.

183

MR M: It was like being in a nightmare. I was trying to get to the school, I knew that if I didn't hurry I was going to be late so I *had to get to the school*... but every road I took was blocked by policemen and soldiers with their guns ready, or Comrades building barricades. First I tried Jabulani Street, then I turned into Kwaza Road and then Lamini Street... and then I gave up and just wandered around aimlessly, helplessly, watching my world go mad and set itself on fire. Everywhere I went... overturned buses, looted bread vans, the Government offices... everything burning and the children dancing around, rattling boxes of matches and shouting Tshisa Qhumisa! Tshisa Qhumisa! Qhumisa!... and then running for their lives when the armoured cars appeared. They were everywhere, crawling around in the smoke like giant dung-beetles looking for shit to eat.

I ended up on the corner where Mrs Makatini always sits selling vetkoek and prickly pears to people waiting for the bus. The only person there was little Sipho Fondini from Standard Six, writing on the wall: "Liberation first, then education." He saw me and called out: "Is the spelling right, Mr M?" And he meant it! The young eyes in that smoke-stained little face were terribly serious. Somewhere else a police van raced past me crowded with children who should have also been at their desks in school. Their hands waved desperately through the bars, their voices called out: "Teacher! Teacher! Help us! Tell our mothers. Tell our fathers." "No, Anela," I said, "this is too much now. Just stand here and close your eyes and wait until you wake up and find your world the way it was." But that didn't happen. A police car came around the corner and suddenly there were children everywhere throwing stones and teargas bombs falling all around and I knew that I wasn't dreaming, that I was coughing and choking and hanging on to a lamp-post in the real world. No! No! Do something, Anela. Do something. Stop the madness! Stop the madness.

MR M *alone in Number One Classroom.*
He is ringing his school bell wildly.

MR M: Come to school! Come to school. Before they kill you all, come to school!

[*Silence.*]

[MR M *looks around the empty classroom. He goes to his table, and after composing himself, opens the class register and reads out the names as he did every morning at the start of a new school day.*]

MR M: Johnny Awu, living or dead? Christopher Bandla, living or dead? Zandile Cwati, living or dead? Semphiwe Dambuza... Ronald Gxasheka... Noloyiso Mfundweni... Stephen Gaika... Zachariah Jabavu... Thami... Thami Mbikwana... [*Pause*] Living or dead?

How many young souls do I have present this morning? There are a lot of well-aimed stray bullets flying around on the streets out there. Is that why this silence is so... heavy?

But what can I teach you? [*Picks up his little black dictionary on the table*] My lessons were meant to help you in *this* world. I wanted you to know how to read and write and talk in *this* world of living, stupid, cruel men.

[*Helpless gesture*] Now? Oh my children! I have no lessons that will be of any use to you now. Mr M and all his wonderful words are... useless, useless, useless!

[*The sound of breaking glass. Stones land in the classroom.* MR M *picks up one*] No! One of you is still alive. Ghosts don't throw stones with hot, sweating young hands. [*Grabs his bell and rings it wildly again*] Come to school! Come to school!

[THAMI *appears.*]

THAMI: [*Quietly*] Stop ringing that bell, Mr M.

MR M: Why? It's only the school bell, Thami. I though you liked the sound of it. You once told me that it was almost as good as music... don't you remember?

THAMI: You are provoking the Comrades with it.

185

MR M: No Thami. I am summoning the Comrades with it.

THAMI: They say you are ringing the bell to taunt them. You are openly defying the boycott by being here in the school.

MR M: I ring this bell because according to my watch it is school time and I am a teacher and those desks are empty! I will go on ringing it as I have been doing these past two weeks, at the end of every lesson. And you can tell the Comrades that I will be back here ringing it tomorrow and the day after tomorrow and for as many days after that as it takes for this world to come to its senses.

Is that the only reason you've come? To tell me to stop ringing the school bell?

THAMI: No.

MR M: You haven't come for a lesson, have you?

THAMI: No I haven't.

MR M: Of course not. What's the matter with me? Slogans don't need much in the way of grammar, do they? As for these . . . [*The stone in his hand*] No, you don't need me for lessons in stone-throwing either. You've already got teachers in those very revolutionary subjects, haven't you? [*Picks up his dictionary . . . the stone in one hand, the book in the other*] You know something interesting, Thami . . . if you put these two on a scale I think you would find that they weighed just about the same. But in this hand I am holding the whole English language. This . . . [*The stone*] . . . is just *one* word in that language. It's true! All that wonderful poetry that you and Isabel tried to cram into your beautiful heads . . . in here! Twenty-six letters, sixty thousand words. The greatest souls the world has ever known were able to open the floodgates of their ecstasy, their despair, their joy! . . . with the words in this little book. Aren't you tempted? I was.

[*Opens the book at the fly-leaf and reads*] Anela Myalatya. Cookhouse. 1947. One of the first books I ever bought. [*Impulsively*] I want you to have it.

THAMI: [*Ignoring the offered book*] I've come here to warn you.

MR M: You've already done that and I've already told you that you are wasting your breath. Now take your stones and go. There are a lot of unbroken windows left.

THAMI: I'm not talking about the bell now. It's more serious than that.

MR M: In my life nothing is more serious than ringing the school bell.

THAMI: There was a meeting last night. Somebody stood up and denounced you as an informer. [*Pause.* THAMI *waits.* MR M *says nothing*] He said you gave names to the police. [MR M *says nothing*]

Everybody is talking about it this morning. You are in big danger.

MR M: Why are you telling me all this?

THAMI: So that you can save yourself. There's a plan to march to the school and burn it down. If they find you here...
[*Pause*]

MR M: Go on. [*Violently*] If they find me here, *what*?

THAMI: They will kill you.

MR M: "They will kill me." That's better. Remember what I taught you... if you've got a problem put it into words so that you can look at it, handle it and ultimately solve it. They will kill me! You are right. That is very serious. So then... what must I do? Must I run away and hide somewhere?

THAMI: No, they will find you. You must join the boycott.

MR M: I'm listening.

THAMI: Let me go back and tell them that we have had a long talk and that you have realised you were wrong and have decided to join us. Let me say that you will sign the declaration and that you won't have anything to do with the school until all demands have been met.

MR M: And they will agree to that? Accept me as one of them even though it is believed that I am an informer?

THAMI: I will tell them you are innocent. That I confronted you with the charge and that you denied it and that I believe you.

MR M: I see. [*Studying* THAMI *intently*] *You* don't believe that I am an informer.

THAMI: No.

MR M: Won't you be taking a chance in defending me like that? Mightn't they end up suspecting you?

THAMI: They'll believe me. I'll make them believe me.

MR M: You can't be sure. Mobs don't listen to reason, Thami. Hasn't your revolution already taught you that? Why take a chance like that to save a collaborator? Why do you want to do all this for me?

THAMI: [*Avoiding* MR M'S *eyes*] I'm not doing it for you. I'm doing it for the Struggle. Our Cause will suffer if we falsely accuse and hurt innocent people.

MR M: I see. My 'execution' would be an embarrassment to the Cause. I apologise, Thami. For a moment I allowed myself to think that you were doing it because we were... who we are... the "all-knowing Mr M and his brilliant protégé Thami!" I was so proud of us when Isabel called us that. Well, young Comrade, you have got nothing to worry about. Let them come and do whatever it is they want to. Your Cause won't be embarrassed, because you see, they won't be 'hurting' an innocent man. [*He makes his confession simply and truthfully.*] That's right, Thami. I am guilty. I did go to the police. I sat down in Captain Lategan's office and told him I felt it was my duty to report the presence in our community of strangers from the north. I told him that I had reason to believe that they were behind the present unrest. I gave the Captain names and addresses. He thanked me and offered me money for the information which I refused. [*Pause*] Why do you look at me like that? Isn't that what you expected from me?... a government stooge, a sell-out, an arse-licker? Isn't that what you were all secretly hoping I would do... so that you could be proved right? [*Appalled*] Is that why I did it? Out of spite? Can a man destroy himself, his life for a reason as petty as that? I sat here before going to the police station saying to myself that it was my duty, to my conscience, to you, to the whole community, to do whatever I could to put an end to this madness of boycotts and arson, mob violence and lawlessness... and maybe that is true... but only maybe... because Thami, the truth is that I was so lonely! You had deserted me. I was so jealous of those who had taken you away. *Now*, I've *really* lost you, haven't I? Yes. I can see it in your eyes. You'll never forgive me for doing that, will you?

You know, Thami, I'd sell my soul to have you all back behind your desks for one last lesson. Yes. If the devil thought it was worth having and offered me that in exchange... one lesson!... he could have my soul. So then it's all over! Because this... [*The classroom*] is all there was for me. This was my home, my life, my one and only ambition... to be a good teacher!

[*His dictionary*] Anela Myalatya, twenty years old, from Cookhouse, wanted to be that the way your friends want to be big soccer stars playing for Kaiser Chiefs! That ambition goes back to when he was just a skinny little ten-year-old pissing on a small grey bush at the top of the Wapadsberg Pass.

We were on our way to a rugby match at Somerset East. The lorry stopped at the top of the mountain so that we could stretch our legs and relieve ourselves. It was a hard ride on the back of that lorry. The road hadn't been tarred yet. So there I was, ten years old and sighing with relief as I aimed for the little bush. It was a hot day. The sun right over our heads... not a cloud in a vast blue sky. I looked up... it's very high up there at the top of the pass... and there it was, stretching away from the foot of the mountain, the great pan of the Karoo... stretching away for ever, it seemed, into the purple haze and heat of the horizon. Something grabbed my heart at that moment, my soul, and squeezed it until there were tears in my eyes. I had never seen anything so big, so beautiful in all my life. I went to the teacher who was with us and asked him: "Teacher, where will I come to if I start walking that way?"... and I pointed. He laughed. "Little man," he said, "that way is North. If you start walking that way and just keep on walking, and your legs don't give in, you will see all of Africa! Yes, Africa, little man! You will see the great rivers of the continent: The Vaal, the Zambesi, the Limpopo, the Congo and then the mighty Nile. You will see the mountains: the Drakensberg, Kilimanjaro, Kenya and the Ruwenzori. And you will meet all our brothers: the little Pygmies of the forests, the proud Masai, the Watusi...tallest of the tall, and the Kikuyu standing on

189

one leg like herons in a pond waiting for a frog." "Has teacher seen all that?" I asked. "No," he said. "Then how does teacher know it's there?" "Because it is all in the books and I have read the books and if you work hard in school, little man, you can do the same without worrying about your legs giving in."

He was right, Thami. *I* have seen it. It is all there in the books just as he said it was and I have made it mine. I can stand on the banks of all those great rivers, look up at the majesty of all those mountains, whenever I want to. It is a journey I have made many times. Whenever my spirit was low and I sat alone in my room, I said to myself: Walk, Anela! Walk!... and I imagined myself at the foot of the Wapadsberg setting off for that horizon that called me that day forty years ago. It always worked! When I left that little room, I walked back into the world a proud man, because I was an African and all the splendour was my birthright. [*Pause*]

I don't want to make that journey again, Thami. There is someone waiting for me now at the end of it who has made a mockery of all my visions of splendour. He has in his arms my real birthright. I saw him on the television in the Reverend Mbopa's lounge. An Ethiopian tribesman, and he was carrying the body of a little child that had died of hunger in the famine... a small bundle carelessly wrapped in a few rags. I couldn't tell how old the man was. The lines of despair and starvation on his face made him look as old as Africa itself.

He held that little bundle very lightly as he shuffled along to a mass grave, and when he reached it, he didn't have the strength to kneel and lay it down gently... He just opened his arms and let it fall. I was very upset when the programme ended. Nobody had thought to tell us his name and whether he was the child's father, or grandfather, or uncle. And the same for the baby! Didn't it have a name? How dare you show me one of our children being thrown away and not tell me its name! I demand to know who is in that bundle! [*Pause*]

Not knowing their names doesn't matter any more. They

190

are more than just themselves. That tribesman and dead child do duty for all of us, Thami. Every African soul is either carrying that bundle or in it.

What is wrong with this world that it wants to waste you all like that... my children... my Africa!

[*Holding out a hand as if he wanted to touch* THAMI'S *face*] My beautiful and proud young Africa!

[*More breaking glass and stones and the sound of a crowd outside the school.* MR M *starts to move.* THAMI *stops him.*]

THAMI: No! Don't go out there. Let me speak to them first. Listen to me! I will tell them I have confronted you with the charges and that you have denied them and that I believe you. I will tell them you are innocent.

MR M: You will lie for me, Thami?

THAMI: Yes.

MR M: [*Desperate to hear the truth*] Why?

[THAMI *can't speak.*]

MR M: Why will you lie for me, Thami?

THAMI: I've told you before.

MR M: The 'Cause'?

THAMI: Yes.

MR M: Then I do not need to hide behind your lies.

THAMI: They will kill you.

MR M: Do you think I'm frightened of them? Do you think I'm frightened of dying?

[MR M *breaks away from* THAMI. *Ringing his bell furiously he goes outside and confronts the mob. They kill him.*]

SCENE 4

THAMI *waiting.*

ISABEL *arrives.*

THAMI: Isabel.

ISABEL: [*It takes her a few seconds to respond*] Hello, Thami.

THAMI: Thank you for coming.

ISABEL: [*She is tense. Talking to him is not easy*] I wasn't going to. Let me tell you straight out that there is nothing in this world... nothing!... that I want to see less at this

191

moment than anything or anybody from the location. But you said in your note that it was urgent, so here I am. If you've got something to say I'll listen.

THAMI: Are you in a hurry?

ISABEL: I haven't got to be somewhere else, if that's what you mean. But if you're asking because it looks as if I would like to run away from here, from you!... very fast, then the answer is yes. But don't worry, I'll be able to control that urge for as long as you need to say what you want to.

THAMI: [*Awkward in the face of* ISABEL'S *severe and unyielding attitude*] I just wanted to say goodbye.

ISABEL: Again?

THAMI: What do you mean?

ISABEL: You've already done that, Thami. Maybe you didn't use that word, but you turned your back on me and walked out of my life that last afternoon the three of us... [*She can't finish*]

How long ago was that?

THAMI: Three weeks, I think.

ISABEL: So why do you want to do it again? Aren't you happy with that last time? It was so dramatic, Thami!

THAMI: [*Patiently*] I wanted to see you because I'm leaving the town, I'm going away for good.

ISABEL: Oh I see. This is meant to be a 'sad' goodbye, is it? [*She is on the edge*] I'm sorry if I'm hurting your feelings but I thought you wanted to see me because you had something to say about recent events in our little community... [*Out of a pocket a crumpled little piece of newspaper which she opens with unsteady hands*] ... a certain unrest-related... I think that is the phrase they use... yes... here it is... [*Reading*] "... unrest-related incident in which according to witnesses the defenceless teacher was attacked by a group of blacks who struck him over the head with an iron rod before setting him on fire."

THAMI: Stop it, Isabel!

ISABEL: [*Fighting hard for self-control*] Oh Thami, I wish I could! I've tried everything, but nothing helps. It just keeps going around and around inside my head. I've tried crying. I've tried praying! I've even tried confrontation. Ja, the day

192

after it happened I tried to get into the location. I wanted to find the witnesses who reported it so accurately and ask them: Why didn't you stop it! There was a police roadblock at the entrance and they wouldn't let me in. They thought I was crazy or something and 'escorted' me back into the safekeeping of two now very frightened parents.

There is nothing wrong with me! All I need is someone to tell me why he was killed. What madness drove those people to kill a man who had devoted his whole life to helping them? He was such a good man, Thami! He was one of the most beautiful human beings I have ever known and his death is one of the ugliest things I have ever known.

THAMI: [*Gives her a few seconds to calm down. Gently*] He was an informer, Isabel. Somehow or the other somebody discovered that Mr M was an informer.

ISABEL: You mean that list of pupils taking part in the boycott? You call that informing?

THAMI: No. It was worse than that. He went to the police and gave them the names and addresses of our political action committee. All of them were arrested after his visit. They are now in detention.

ISABEL: Mr M did that?

THAMI: Yes.

ISABEL: I don't believe it.

THAMI: It's true, Isabel.

ISABEL: No! What proof do you have?

THAMI: His own words. He told me so himself. I didn't believe it either when he was first accused, but the last time I saw him, he said it was true, that he had been to the police.

ISABEL: [*Stunned disbelief*] Mr M? A police spy? For how long?

THAMI: No. It wasn't like that. He wasn't paid or anything. He went to the police just that one time. He said he felt it was his duty.

ISABEL: What do you mean?

THAMI: Operation Qhumisa ... the boycotts and strikes, the arson ... you know he didn't agree with any of that. But he was also very confused about it all. I think he wished

193

he had never done it.

ISABEL: So he went to the police just once?

THAMI: Yes.

ISABEL: And as a matter of conscience?

THAMI: Yes.

ISABEL: That doesn't make him an 'informer', Thami!

THAMI: Then what do you call somebody who gives information to the police?

ISABEL: No! You know what that word really means, the sort of person it suggests. Was Mr M one of those? He was acting out of concern for his people... you said so yourself. He thought he was doing the right thing! You don't murder a man for that!

THAMI: [*Near the end of his patience*] Be careful, Isabel.

ISABEL: Of what?

THAMI: The words you use.

ISABEL: Oh? Which one don't you like? Murder? What do you want me to call it... 'an unrest-related incident'? If you are going to call him an informer, then I am going to call his death murder!

THAMI: It was an act of self-defence.

ISABEL: By who?

THAMI: The People.

ISABEL: [*Almost speechless with outrage*] What? A mad mob attacks one unarmed defenceless man and you want me to call it...

THAMI: [*Abandoning all attempts at patience. He speaks with the full authority of the anger inside him.*] Stop, Isabel! You just keep quiet now and listen to me. You're always saying you want to understand us and what it means to be black... well if you do, listen to me carefully now. I don't call it murder, and I don't call the people who did it a mad mob and yes, I do expect you to see it as an act of self-defence... listen to me!... blind and stupid but still self-defence.

He betrayed us and our fight for freedom. Five men are in detention because of Mr M's visit to the police station. There have been other arrests and there will be more. Why do you think I'm running away?

194

How were those people to know he wasn't a paid informer who had been doing it for a long time and would do it again? They were defending themselves against what they thought was a terrible danger to themselves. What Anela Myalatya did to them and their cause is what your laws define as treason when it is done to you and threatens the safety and security of your comfortable white world. Anybody accused of it is put on trial in your courts and if found guilty they get hanged. Many of my people have been found guilty and have been hanged. Those hangings *we* call murder!

Try to understand, Isabel. Try to imagine what it is like to be a black person, choking inside with rage and frustration, bitterness, and then to discover that one of your own kind is a traitor, has betrayed you to those responsible for the suffering and misery of your family, of your people. What would you do? Remember there is no magistrate or court you can drag him to and demand that he be tried for that crime.

There is no justice for black people in this country other than what we make for ourselves. When you judge us for what happened in front of the school four days ago just remember that you carry a share of the responsibility for it. It is your laws that have made simple, decent black people so desperate that they turn into 'mad mobs'.

[ISABEL *has been listening and watching intently. It looks as if she is going to say something, but she stops herself*] Say it, Isabel.

ISABEL: No.

THAMI: This is your last chance. You once challenged me to be honest with you. I'm challenging you now.

ISABEL: [*She faces him*] Were you there when it happened, Thami? [*Pause*] And if you were, did you try to stop them?

THAMI: Isn't there a third question, Isabel? Was I one of the mob that killed him?

ISABEL: Yes. Forgive me, Thami... please forgive me!... but there is that question as well. Only once! Believe me, only once... late at night when I couldn't sleep. I couldn't believe it was there in my head, but I heard the words...

195

"Was Thami one of the ones who did it?"

THAMI: If the police catch me, that's the question they will ask.

ISABEL: I'm asking you because... [*An open, helpless gesture*] ... I'm lost! I don't know what to think or feel any more. Help me. Please. You're the only one who can. Nobody else seems to understand that I loved him.

[*This final confrontation is steady and unflinching on both sides.*]

THAMI: Yes, I was there. Yes, I did try to stop it. [THAMI *gives* ISABEL *time to deal with this answer.*] I knew how angry the people were. I went to warn him. If he had listened to me he would still be alive, but he wouldn't. It was almost as if he wanted it to happen. I think he hated himself very much for what he had done, Isabel. He kept saying to me that it was all over. He was right. There was nothing left for him. That visit to the police station had finished everything. Nobody would have ever spoken to him again or let him teach their children.

ISABEL: Oh Thami, it is all so wrong! So stupid! That's what I can't take... the terrible stupidity of it. We needed him. All of us.

THAMI: I know.

ISABEL: Then why is he dead?

THAMI: You must stop asking these questions, Isabel. You know the answers.

ISABEL: They don't make any sense, Thami.

THAMI: I know what you are feeling. [*Pause*] I also loved him. Doesn't help much to say it now I know, but I did. Because he made me angry and impatient with his 'old-fashioned' ideas, I didn't want to admit it. Even if I had, it wouldn't have stopped me from doing what I did, the boycott and everything, but I should have tried harder to make him understand why I was doing it. You were right about that. Now...? [*A helpless gesture*] You know the most terrible words in your language, Isabel? Too late.

ISABEL: Ja.

THAMI: I'll never forgive myself for not trying harder with him and letting him know... my true feelings for him. Right

196

until the end I tried to deny it . . . to him, to myself.

ISABEL: I'm sorry I . . .

THAMI: That's all right.

ISABEL: Are the police really looking for you?

THAMI: Yes. Some of my friends have already been detained. They're pulling in anybody they can get their hands on.

ISABEL: Where are you going? Cape Town?

THAMI: No. That's the first place they'll look. I've written to my parents telling them about everything. I'm heading north.

ISABEL: To where?

THAMI: Far Isabel. I am leaving the country.

ISABEL: Does that mean what I think it does?

THAMI: [*He nods*] I'm going to join the movement. I want to be a fighter. I've been thinking about it for a long time. Now I know it's the right thing to do. I don't want to end up being one of the mob that killed Mr M . . . but that will happen to me if I stayed here.

ISABEL: Oh, Thami.

THAMI: I know I'm doing the right thing. Believe me.

ISABEL: I'll try.

THAMI: And you?

ISABEL: I don't know what to do with myself, Thami. All I know is that I'm frightened of losing him. He's only been dead four days and I think I'm already starting to forget what he looked like. But the worst thing is that there's nowhere for me to go and . . . you know . . . just be near him. That's so awful. I got my father to phone the police but they said there wasn't enough left of him to justify a grave. What there was has been disposed of in a 'Christian manner'. So where do I go? The burnt-out ruins of the school? I couldn't face that.

THAMI: Get your father or somebody to drive you to the top of the Wapadsberg Pass. It's on the road to Cradock.

ISABEL: I know it.

THAMI: It was a very special place for him. He told me that it was there where it all started, where he knew what he wanted to do with his life . . . being a teacher, being the 'Mr M' we knew. You'll be near him up there. I must go.

ISABEL: Do you need money?

197

THAMI: No. Sala Kakuhle, Isabel. That's the Xhosa goodbye.
ISABEL: I know. U'sispumla taught me to say it.
Hamba Kakuhle Thami.
[THAMI *leaves.*]

SCENE 5

ISABEL *alone.*
*She stands quietly, examining the silence. After a few seconds
she nods her head slowly.*
ISABEL: Yes! Thami was right, Mr M. He said I'd feel near you up
here.
He's out there somewhere, Mr M... travelling north. He
didn't say where exactly he was going, but I think we can
guess, can't we?
I'm here for a very 'old-fashioned' reason, so I know
you'll approve. I've come to pay my last respects to Anela
Myalatya. I know the old-fashioned way of doing that is
to bring flowers, lay them on the grave, say a quiet prayer
and then go back to your life. But that seemed sort of silly
this time. You'll have enough flowers around here when
spring comes... which it will. So instead I've brought you
something which I know will mean more to you than
flowers or prayers ever could. A promise. I am going to
make Anela Myalatya a promise.
You gave me a little lecture once about wasted lives...
how much of it you'd seen, how much you hated it, how
much you didn't want to happen to Thami and me. I sort
of understood what you meant at the time. Now, I most
certainly do. Your death has seen to that. My promise to
you is that I am going to try as hard as I can, in every
way that I can, to see that it doesn't happen to me. I am
going to try my best to make my life useful in the way that
yours was. I want you to be proud of me. After all, I am
one of your children, you know. You did welcome me to
your family.
[*A pause*] The future is still ours, Mr M.

[*The actor leaves the stage.*]

198